W9-BTF-140

Sharon,

Enjoy the read

2/18/10

Advance Praise for Winning Strategies

Winning large outsourcing deals is not just about mastery in sales. The practice requires excellence in governance, management, finance, negotiation, and the capacity to understand human behavior, among other elements. Anirban and Hetzel highlight this and take us through the numerous aspects of winning large deals.

> —***Raj G Asava***, *Chief Strategy Officer, Perot Systems*

Mega deals are the arteries of the services organization. Nurturing the lead to a deal is a subject of complexity beyond men and machines. This book looks at mega deals from a lifecycle point of view and thus helps everyone understand the situational aspects of deal making through its various stages.

> —***Ed Nair***, *Editor, Global Services*

The perception of large and strategic deals, especially from an off-shoring standpoint, has been ambiguous. This book not only clearly delineates what large deals stand for but also substantiates the strategic long-term benefits of pursuing such deals.

> —***Sridhar Vedala***, *Managing Director, Equaterra*

Now that the benefits of global sourcing are clear for everyone to behold, this book provides the coaching required for sales leaders to really hone their skills and become true professionals!

> —***David Lancashire***, *CEO and Chairman, Bold Ventures*

Successful deal making is both a science and an art, and it is not any different for an outsourcing deal. Offshore outsourcing deals bring their own dimensions and complexities. A book such as this provides insight and experience from all angles and will certainly be a reference book for anyone involved in any and all aspects of mega deals.

> —***Jagdish Dalal***, *President, JDalal Associates*

Big deals require a process that runs from discovery to revenue recognition. This book demonstrates the in-depth understanding of this process required for senior management as well as for the quota carriers.

> —***Ed Peters***, *CEO, OpenConnect Systems*

This is the quintessential guide to best practices in big deal global sourcing. Anyone touching the global outsourcing arena should tap into this tremendous resource.

—**Melissa Henderson**, *Managing Director, Gilbert Tweed International*

This book is an excellent resource for all business development professionals. It has great lessons that can be explored and implemented to help achieve higher goals and benefits for everyone. I highly recommend this read.

—**Ed Cohen**, *Chief Learning Officer at a major IT service company and the author of* Leadership Without Borders

Putting large IT outsourcing deals together is both science and art. This immensely practical book, written by experienced dealmakers, covers both aspects as it walks you through all of the major steps, from finding and winning deals through contract negotiation and deal closing.

—**Vijay Gurbaxani**, *Professor of Information Systems and Computer Science, Paul Merage School of Business, University of California, Irvine*

WINNING STRATEGIES

Secrets to Clinching Multimillion-Dollar Deals

WINNING STRATEGIES

Secrets to Clinching Multimillion-Dollar Deals

Anirban Dutta
and
Hetzel W. Folden

John Wiley & Sons (Asia) Pte. Ltd.

Copyright © 2010 John Wiley & Sons (Asia) Pte. Ltd.

Published in 2010 by John Wiley & Sons (Asia) Pte. Ltd.
2 Clementi Loop, #02-01, Singapore 129809

All rights reserved.

No part of this publication may be reproduced, stored in a retrieval system, or transmitted in any form or by any means, electronic, mechanical, photocopying, recording, scanning, or otherwise, except as expressly permitted by law, without either the prior written permission of the Publisher, or authorization through payment of the appropriate photocopy fee to the Copyright Clearance Center. Requests for permission should be addressed to the Publisher, John Wiley & Sons (Asia) Pte. Ltd., 2 Clementi Loop, #02-01, Singapore 129809, tel: 65-64632400, fax: 65-64646912, e-mail: enquiry@wiley.com.

This publication is designed to provide accurate and authoritative information in regard to the subject matter covered. It is sold with the understanding that the Publisher is not engaged in rendering professional services. If professional advice or other expert assistance is required, the services of a competent professional person should be sought.

Other Wiley Editorial Offices
John Wiley & Sons, Inc., 111 River Street, Hoboken, NJ 07030, USA
John Wiley & Sons, Ltd., The Atrium, Southern Gate, Chichester, West Sussex P019 8SQ, UK
John Wiley & Sons (Canada), Ltd., 5353 Dundas Street West, Suite 400, Toronto, Ontario
   M9B 6H8, Canada
John Wiley & Sons Australia Ltd., 42 McDougall Street, Milton, Queensland 4064, Australia
Wiley-VCH, Boschstrasse 12, D-69469 Weinheim, Germany

Library of Congress Cataloging-in-Publication Data
ISBN: 9780470824665

Typeset in 10.5/13 point, Garamond Light by Thomson Digital
Printed in Singapore by Saik Wah Press Pte. Ltd.
10 9 8 7 6 5 4 3 2 1

Words cannot express the gratitude I have for my wife, Julie. Her editing of the manuscript, singlehandedly looking after our two-year-olds for twelve months so I could focus on the book, and constant moral support have been instrumental in getting this book published. Thanks to my son, Jai, and my daughter, Maya, for helping relieve my stress and bringing incredible joy in my life. Thank you also to my parents, Jayanta and Anjali, who by nature and nurture gave me the ability to complete this book. I dedicate this book to all of you.

Anirban Dutta

To my wife, Cindy, my true partner in life—professional, personal, and spiritual. Without her keen insights and constant consultations, I would be directionless and purposeless. In celebration of our twenty-fifth wedding anniversary, I dedicate this book and my career successes to you.

Hetzel W. Folden

CONTENTS

ACKNOWLEDGMENTS

It is extremely difficult to write acknowledgments because we are certain we will unknowingly forget to credit some people who deserve appreciation for the contents of this book. So at the outset, we sincerely thank everybody, from teachers to colleagues, professional organizations, educational institutions, employers, customers, and everyone in between, from both past and present, that have helped shape our views on Big Deals and global sourcing in general. But we would be ungrateful if we did not mention a few individuals without whom this book would not have become reality.

Ed Cohen, the author of *Leadership Without Borders*, took it on himself to get us connected with John Wiley & Sons. This book would not have happened had he not steered us to the publishers. A big thanks to the entire Wiley team of Nick Wallwork, C. J. Hwu, Janis Soo, Joyce Poh, Fiona Wong, Louise Koh, Cynthia Mak, Jessie Yeo, Camy Boey and others from Wiley Singapore; Paras Bansal and Vikas Gupta from Wiley India; and copy editors Roger Bullen and Thomas Finnegan, who stayed with us as we kept slipping deadlines while pushing the schedule back.

You may be surprised to learn that a lot of expert help for this book came from people who have nothing to do with global sourcing. But these people offered some core values that can be relied on heavily to win Big global sourcing Deals. For example, Mahesh Bhupathi, possibly the only active professional tennis player (11-time Grand Slam doubles champion) who simultaneously runs a multimillion-dollar business, provided us with some valuable insights on how to build relationships at the highest level while maintaining an insane travel schedule. We had a vision about how futuristic structures for outsourcing deals should look. Thanks to Fazal Syed, a derivatives expert from a major U.S. commercial bank; Jeff Noland, investment banker; and Sukh Saluja, international structuring services expert, who lent a hand in putting the framework around those structures applicable to global sourcing deal making. Thanks also to legal expert Sumathi Chandrashekaran (author of the blog *SpicyIP*), who guided us with details regarding complex IP-related lawsuits.

Global sourcing gurus played a great role acting as subject matter experts (SMEs) for this book. Nirmal (Nimma) Bakshi, a senior leader at a major IT services provider, not only gave his views of how alliance-led "go-to-market" models ought to look but also gave us a futuristic roadmap for alliances. Rajesh Venkatraman from IBM offered his point of view on alliance management in Asia. Balu T.*, the head of service delivery for Satyam's infrastructure practice, was kind enough to share his unique views on leadership in his typically funny and sarcastic way. Lori Blackman, founder and CEO of the Dallas-based talent management firm DNL Global, taught us the ins and outs of hiring the best deal team members to fit perfectly in any organization. David Hott, a solutions architect with IBM, was instrumental in furnishing input on how architects can play a leading role in large service delivery once the deal is sold. Mahesh Ramachandran from EDS, who has both buy- and sell-side experience, gave us field-tested tips on how to create an environment where the provider and the customer truly partner one another to get the work done. Ken Green, a 20-year-veteran active reservist with the U.S. Air Force and also transition manager for Accenture, simplified transition management by drawing parallels between managing a team in combat and an IT services transition team. Terrence Shaw, CEO of the IT services company Wirevibe, helped to come up with practical case studies on how and why major global service providers run into pitfalls in service delivery engagement. Sandip Bhattachaya, program manager in Satyam, shared with us his creation—the "person commitment and capability model"—a practical and easy-to-use model to manage large IT service delivery programs. Sergey Shneyerson, a Kellogg MBA heading Mirantis's U.S. sales, shared with us a sales model with which he can outcompete Indian pure plays and take work to Russia. An old sales warhorse, Brent Davidson, shared his secrets of consistently growing Big Deals in penetrated accounts. A mega thanks to Dallas's own third-party advisor expert Tom Tunstall for helping out with dissecting the complex world of TPAs. And last but not least, a *big* thanks to all of Hetzel's Strategic Deals Group (SDG) at Satyam and his current team at Computer Sciences Corporation (CSC), who live day in and day out by the principles defined in this book.

---

*It is a common practice in the southern parts of India to use the first name and initial of the last name as the full name. We have referred to Balu's name in that format because he prefers to be called Balu T.

Seasoned executives taught us more than a thing or two along the way. Pioneer Natural Resources CIO Tom Halbouty told us how important it is for providers to have full control of subvendors. He helped us understand how to manage risk and showcase that risk management ability to CIOs to win deals. Sudhakar Gorti, a former VP at NBC with operational directives, helped us understand the COO mind-set. Ted Ehling, CEO of Balanced Performance, helped us with a master stroke in account development strategies. Thanks to Sunil Maheshwari, CEO of Mango Technologies, for sharing with us how to create a culture where salespeople behave as though they are poor, hungry, and driven to win deals.

Reviewing is harder than writing in many ways. We reserve special thanks for our reviewers. The book went through several iterations as the English being used was analyzed and critiqued by the academic father-daughter duo of Frank Markus and Julie Dutta. Nandan Das took time off from designing satellite systems at Viasat by doing a thorough end-to-end, word-by-word review of the book. His acute reasoning and non-sugar-coated comments about the original version of the book have undoubtedly increased the overall quality.

Special thanks go to a list of esteemed technology luminaries, notably Kiran Karnik, former president of the National Association of Software and Services Companies (NASSCOM) and chairman of the board at a major IT services provider; Michael Corbett, chairman of International Association of Outsourcing Professionals (IAOP); Tim Cummins, president and CEO of International Association of Contracts and Commercial Management (IACCM); Russ Owen, president of Managed Services Sector at Computer Sciences Corporation (CSC); David Mitchell, senior vice president at Ovum Consulting; and Frank Casale, founder and CEO of the Outsourcing Institute. They offered their public endorsement for the back cover of the book.

Further thanks go to outsourcing experts Raj Asava, chief strategy officer at Perot Systems; Ed Nair, editor of Global Services Media; Sridhar Vedala, former managing director at Equaterra; David Lancashire, chairman and CEO of Bold Ventures; Jagdish Dalal, renowned thought leader of outsourcing and CEO of JDalal Associates; Ed Peters, CEO of OpenConnect Systems; Melissa Henderson, managing director at Gilbert Tweed International; Ed Cohen; and Vijay Gurbaxani, professor of information systems and computer science at the Paul Merage School of Business, University of California, Irvine. They all took the time to review the book and provide us their comments on the content.

We want to thank our employer, CSC, for supporting us in getting this book published. We are also pleased that the Foreword was written by two global sourcing pioneers, Doug Brown and Scott Wilson, who are coauthors of the best-selling business book *The Black Book of Outsourcing: How to Manage the Changes, Challenges and Opportunities* (Wiley, 2005, 2008). Thanks, Doug and Scott! Your endorsement means a lot to us.

We cannot conclude the acknowledgments without thanking our spouses, Julie and Cindy, for being with us through this entire journey. Your personal sacrifices help us become better deal makers. And finally, big thanks go to all our readers. We really hope that this book will help you in getting some value while doing deals.

Thanks.
—Anirban Dutta and Hetzel W. Folden

FOREWORD

This book should come with a warning label:

Caution: Do not read this book if you're the least bit apprehensive about huge successes or the thrills of enormous global opportunities.

Genuine deal makers will find themselves absolutely inspired, motivated, and empowered to passionate extremes as this book's principles unfold.

The new world economy has opened up a schism between imagining win-win deals and actually structuring them. The process requires a management skill set far beyond hard work and strategic aptitude. Few have attempted it, and far fewer have successfully mastered the craft.

Two of the gifted masters, Anirban Dutta and Hetzel Folden, offer up their global market expertise for strategic deal making as a new generation of business leaders evolves to understand vital outsourcing solutions.

The art and science of contemporary deal making has had no better laboratory in the growth of the outsourcing industry. Since we first published *The Black Book of Outsourcing: How to Manage the Changes, Challenges and Opportunities* (Wiley) in 2005, most of the Fortune 2000 and Inc. 500's largest organizations have gone through several cycles of outsourcing exercise.

Nowadays, the customers are aided by analysts, advisors, and legal experts in finding the right sourcing partners. By contrast, offshore-based service providers, once regarded simply as low-cost providers suitable for the deals, have stepped up their game and won many Big Deals. Several offshore providers have even crossed the billion-dollar-revenue mark. Traditional large outsourcing companies, which were once viewed as big enough to win Big Deals but not nimble enough to win small deals, have started outcompeting many offshore-based providers at these smaller deals. The outsourcing playing field has been leveled to a great extent.

To make things more complicated, the world has been hit with an unprecedented economic crisis that pundits are saying could last for a few more years. Customers will have to rethink their strategies about operations and sales and eventually become leaner and meaner in order to survive and thrive going forward. We believe that outsourcing opportunities will increase tremendously in the next few years because of explicit customer needs. Who will win the Big Deals in this turbulent yet promising marketplace? Will it be traditional offshore organizations, or will it be the established global system integrators?

Regardless of who wins market share, competition to win outsourcing deals will be harder than ever. The companies that win the deals will be the ones able to get all parts of their organization in sync and follow a thorough end-to-end strategic pursuit process.

Winning Strategies: Secrets to Clinching Multimillion-Dollar Deals is the only book on the market that is focused on end-to-end strategic pursuit process designed toward winning Big Deals in the global marketplace. Anirban and Hetzel have been successful in taking a fairly heavy topic and presenting it as an informative yet light read that is filled with practical anecdotes. The style of writing has made this book appealing for established outsourcing leaders and laypersons alike. The book will encourage deal makers to be students of the market and be selective in choosing pursuits. The book will also challenge human resources leaders in service provider organizations to think about whether their hiring practices augment a holistic deal-winning model. The matter-of-fact tips and discussions on how service providers can find Big Deals, creatively craft and win Big Deals from scratch, and work with third party advisors to align with customer needs, all the while managing bloated egos and organizational politics, will come in handy as outsourcing sales teams pursue Big Deal opportunities. This book offers a very practical take on what we believe are the three most crucial aspects of Big Deal making: structuring, contracting, and negotiating.

Finally, unlike most sales books, this one encourages outsourcing leaders to view transition and service delivery as an extension of the sales process. As you read this book, we encourage you to keep your mind open and try some of its suggestions in your organization.

Doug Brown and Scott Wilson
Coauthors of the best-selling business book The Black Book of Outsourcing: How to Manage the Changes, Challenges and Opportunities *(Wiley, 2005, 2008) and founders of Brown-Wilson Group, an international outsourcing industry research firm.*
www.TheBlackBookOfOutsourcing.com

A Note from the Authors

In December 2008, as we were going through the editing of this book, it seemed as if all hell broke loose for everyone associated with our employer at that time, Satyam Computer Services. On December 16, the Satyam board of directors announced a US$1.6 billion acquisition intended to diversify the firm's businesses. This diversification into non-information-technology businesses was not well received by investors, who reacted negatively, causing a 50 percent decline in the Satyam stock price. The proposed deal was immediately rescinded by Satyam, but not without significant consequences. As of year end 2008, four independent directors of the Satyam board had resigned. Many fingers were pointed at corporate governance. To make matters worse, additional news articles appeared regarding a ban from doing business with the World Bank.

To our shock, this bad phase for Satyam was just the beginning. On January 7, 2009, the chairman resigned from his post, admitting to fraud. He said that the company's cash and balance sheet were inflated and fudged to the tune of US$1.4 billion. Subsequently, both Chairman Ramalinga Raju and his brother Rama Raju (the CEO) were arrested by the Hyderabad police. Satyam became a household name worldwide—in a negative way. News channels from New Delhi to New York covered the Satyam scam in detail, dubbing the company the Enron of India. The stock took a further beating; employee morale went down. There were significant concerns about the company making payroll in January 2009. The government of India stepped in, disbanded the existing board, and formed a new board of directors. This new board basically took control of day-to-day operations. By the middle of February, the board had appointed A. S. Murthy (whom we will call ASM) as CEO from inside Satyam. At the time of editing this book, we were faced with one main question: Would Satyam survive?

We were seriously questioned by some reviewers as to whether it made sense to publish a book on the process of global sourcing of Big Deals in this sickened worldwide business climate. Many people also advised us to wait and publish the book in a year or two, because our association with the Satyam brand could possibly erode some of our credibility about our knowledge of Big Deals.

We decided to go ahead and publish the book as per the original plan. The winning strategies for closing Big Deals presented in this book are still viable, regardless of the state of the economy or some level of corporate fraud. We believe that in a down economy it is extremely important to be nearly perfect in all aspects of deal-making execution. Service delivery organizations will not have the latitude to mess up in sales, delivery, or the core components of deal structuring. We think this down economy gives an added incentive for our potential readers to take up this book and apply its core principles.

Throughout the book, you will see us in some places refer to ourselves as if we are still Satyam employees, although we are no longer part of Satyam. We decided not to change the verbiage. Having written part of this book while working at Satyam, we felt that if we changed the tune of the writing it would dilute the essence of the book. Satyam hired high-end deal makers from the market, focused on winning Big Deals as an organization, and built a process-oriented framework to chase and win deals. The core value of the company cannot be tarnished because of the few men who were responsible for Satyam's downfall, men who ran it from the top. Regardless of the fate of Satyam going forward, we acknowledge that our experience at the company made us better deal makers. We have benefitted from the opportunity to grow our deal-making capabilities in the several Big Deals we worked on at Satyam. Our readers are beneficiaries of that acquired knowledge.

Who Will This Book Benefit?

The editors at Wiley repeatedly asked us to classify this book. Is it a how-to book? A textbook? We feel that it is neither a pure how-to nor a textbook proper, but more of a "journey" book on Big Deals, covering our collective experience along with others' on many aspects—such as hiring, team building, sales, leadership, deal making, negotiation, transition, and governance—that are required to make Big Deals happen. We believe that this book will be a beneficial read for multiple audiences:

- *Casual business book readers* Many people we run into in our extensive global traveling are from completely different professions from the world of global sourcing. They are very curious to know how global sourcing providers such as IBM, HP, and Indian Out-sourcing Providers go and win these Big Deals they hear about in the news. We hope this book will present a broad overview of the entire Big Deals pursuit process that a service provider follows.

- *Deal makers* The experienced deal makers reading the book may resonate with our ideas ("been there, done that"). The book should bring a chuckle to a few novice deal makers who read in disbelief about the organizational politics, behind-the-scenes boardroom antics, and subtle maneuverings of key executives, all in the spirit of closing the Big Deals.
- *Students* We hope to inject enough curiosity through this book for today's business and technology students to want to further investigate career options in the world of global sourcing deal making.
- *IT and other technology professionals* We have seen IT and other technology professionals reach a point in their career where they want to do something else, such as management or sales. This book should give these people who are pondering a career choice thoughts about a high-paying, visible role in the deal-making business.

The bottom line is that the journey you will take, in the pages that follow, will furnish you with a roadmap of how to increase the probability of winning Big Deals and growing your business.

How Is This Book Organized?

We have divided the book into four broad sections that we believe are important in winning large deals. These are the four phases of deal making generally:

Creating the foundation for winning deals → Finding deals → Doing deals → Managing deals

Then we formulate chapters within each section extolling the value of our experience, lessons learned, and words of wisdom from other experts in the field.

Section One: Creating the Foundation for Winning Deals An organization serious about winning Big Deals needs first to create the foundation to win those deals.

Chapter One: "What's the Big Deal? A Primer on Strategic Deals" An introduction to Big Deals in the context of outsourcing. We explore the market outlook on Big Deals. The goal is for you to understand why Big Deals are important and what you need to do in order to pursue them. This chapter also touches on an omnipresent element of every deal maker's toolkit: effectively managing politics to get things done.

Chapter Two: "Getting the Right People Ready to Win Large Deals: Introducing Some Essential Concepts of the Human Element of Management" Acknowledges the fact that once the basics have been understood comes the most important aspect: people. The brightest and savviest of deal makers often fail to win deals because the rest of the organization is pulling them down. Deals cannot be won just by ramping up the deals team with good people. The whole organization needs to be in sync. Hiring for roles is not good enough anymore. Organizations need to view their HR portfolio like a financial portfolio, with varied skills and personalities that complement one another. This chapter explores how organizational hiring needs to be done in order to win Big Deals.

Section Two: Finding Deals Building the foundation is a start. But to win deals, one needs to find them. Section Two is all about finding and creating deals.

Chapter Three: "Finding Big Deals: Strategies to Discover High-Value Deals" Explores the most common question asked by sellers: "Where do I find Big Deals?" This chapter promotes two main ways of finding them: growing within established accounts, and finding deals through new business development activities. The organization and individual best practices that are needed to excel in this category are highlighted here. This chapter also focuses on sales leadership because most growth agendas require sales excellence.

Chapter Four: "Winning Deals Through Third Party Advisors: The Art of People Doing Business with People" All about third party advisors. TPAs are an integral part of the deals ecosystem. Customers rely on them to select providers. How does one court TPAs, and what should one not do? How do TPAs decide to whom to award the deals? Answers to these questions and others are explored.

Section Three: Doing Deals The crux of the book. Once deals are identified, how does an organization close them?

Chapter Five: "Leading from the Rear: Influence Events and Lead the Deal" Deal makers need to become experts at leading from the background. They must be experts in managing organization politics, aligning or severing ties (if need be) with business-unit leaders by being non-confrontational, and most important, able to make key game-changing decisions that make or break Big Deals. The hardest part is that they almost always have to work without enjoying the limelight. Specific traits for leading from the rear are described here.

Chapter Six: "Structuring Deals Right: The Art of Pricing" The territory of Big Deal engagement models and pricing. This is the most important chapter from the point of view of a service provider's CFO office. How should I price this deal? What's the best way this deal can be structured so that I will get my desired profitability? How can I be creative in these deals so I can beat my competitors? Pricing strategies appropriate for winning Big Deals are discussed, along with a synopsis of the whole pricing process.

Chapter Seven: "Advanced Deal Structuring: Creating Innovative Engagement Models and Being Customer Financiers" Advanced deal structuring. Today, we are in a unique situation. Many technology providers have a strong balance sheet whereas their largest customers are more likely than not going bankrupt. Think of Bear Stearns, AIG, and others. But this situation also opened up a great opportunity for service providers. Customers need to do Big Deals so they can transform themselves to stay competitive. Providers need to behave like investment banks and fund customers to do deals. This chapter discusses advanced deal structuring, where old rules are broken and new structures are essential.

Chapter Eight: "Doing Contracts Right: Creating the Foundation of a Successful Marriage" May not sound exciting, but contracts are the factor that really counts most, at least in the eyes of the law. Commitments, outcomes, and expectations are defined in the contract phase and put on paper. This is where the dotted line is signed. Here, we go through common contract terms such as MSA and LSA, and what needs to be in every document (the dos and don'ts of commercial contracts). We also explore how you, as a service provider, can not only assure customers of saving their intellectual property (IP) but bargain for a piece of it as well.

Chapter Nine: "Closing Big Deals: It's Commercial Negotiation, Baby!" Goes hand in hand with the preceding chapter. Providers spend a significant amount of time negotiating with the customer line item by line item. Here we discuss the emotional elements of closing the deal, which are as important as the elements actually written into contracts. Deal makers need to excel in negotiation as part of closing deals.

Chapter Ten: "Case Study: A Real-Life Example of a Service Provider Pursuing Strategic Deals" A step-by-step case study on how a real-life service delivery provider pursues Big Deals. The goal here is for deal makers working for different service providers to get some ideas on creating a Big Deals pursuit process, and their own processes for their organization if need be.

Section Four: Managing Deals It is a myth that you walk away when the deal is won. The reality is that major revenue usually is recognized only in year two or three of the deal's lifetime. This section contains two important post-deal-closing chapters that are an integral part of achieving your desired profitability.

Chapter Eleven: "Managing Transitions and Change: The Stepping Stones for Delivering Service" Talks about change and transition. The Big Deals always have one very important element baked into them as a criterion for success. This is transition, where work is transferred from a customer to a provider, or in many cases from a provider to another provider. A bad transition can absolutely kill a provider in terms of P&L efficiency and customer satisfaction. This chapter describes best practices in transitions.

Chapter Twelve: "Managing Integrated Programs: A Practical Take on Service Delivery Governance" The overarching chapter on governance. We view governance as the ability to keep tabs on every aspect of the deal. We show proven tools and strategies for assessing customer needs and creating a simple yet powerful governance framework. We also focus on how program managers should operate if they want to manage a Big Deal successfully.

Because our target audience is broad, we have decided to keep a conversational tone throughout this book. We have also used many personal examples not related to global sourcing to convey our thoughts and philosophies so that this book does not become a heavy, unread management tome gathering dust on the shelf. As you go through this book, you will see that in some places we give actual names of individuals or businesses, and in other places we refer to them without explicitly naming them. Where we omit the names it is because the people or institutions referred to do not wish to be identified and we respect their privacy.

The book uses some industry-related jargon. We have done our best to explain the terms or expand them wherever we felt it appropriate. But we do realize that because of our broad readership base, some people might need more clarity in really understanding those terms. We pondered building a glossary to clarify common phrases. But then we realized that in today's technology-enabled world, we could guide our readers to find common industry jargon just as we experienced deal makers do. Our best advice to readers wanting to know more about what certain terms of jargon mean is to Google them to get a broad set of hits explaining them. Trust us: experienced deal makers also Google regularly to clarify industry-specific terms.

Last but not least, we want to thank you for picking up this book. So without further ado, happy reading!

CREATING THE FOUNDATION
FOR WINNING DEALS

CHAPTER 1

What's the Big Deal?

A Primer on Strategic Deals

Selected Big Deal Headlines, 1999–2007

Hetzel W. Folden

Hetzel W. Folden

- Aerospace and defense giant Raytheon awards major IT outsourcing contract to Computer Sciences Corporation (CSC); contract estimated at nearly US$2 billion (1999)[1]
- CSC receives US$100 million contract to manage the IT environment at Children's Hospital of Los Angeles (2001)[2]
- Motorola awards US$1.6 billion deal to CSC to outsource infrastructure services (2003)[3]
- BT Concert, a British Telecom and ATT US joint venture, enter into an agreement with CSC to manage the venture's IT applications (2003)[4]
- Ascension Health, the largest Catholic hospital system in the United States, awards IT deal to CSC projected at more than US$1 billion (2004)[5]
- Satyam wins major contract for share of Citigroup's NAIT applications portfolio (2006)[6]
- Satyam wins big deal down under: Qantas Airlines outsources applications work (2007)[7]
- Reuters undertakes major business transformation; Satyam receives ten-year contract worth nearly US$300 million of new business (2007)[8]

What's a Big Global Sourcing Deal?

The first and foremost understanding of closing a large outsourcing (preferably called global sourcing, because we are theoretically professing use of the best resources from all over the world) deal is to recognize that it is a team accomplishment. We often hear the question, "What's the biggest deal you closed?" The editors at Wiley asked us the same question when we were discussing the need for this book. All of the deals mentioned in the headlines above are part of our legacy in closing large global sourcing deals. But it is a colossal overstatement to say that the Big Deals mentioned earlier were closed just because of our individual merits. The wins, as in any Big Deal, were completely a result of teamwork. It is therefore the thesis of this book that we have taken the hard work of many, from within and outside our industry, and boiled it down to a collection of conclusions and lessons learned from "living the deals."

A Big Deal is generally viewed as US$50 million or more in total contract value (TCV). TCV is the sum of all contracted revenue over the

Total, All Deals (US$)	January to October 2008 Total	
	Total No. of Deals	Total Contract Value in US$ Billion
Contracts ≥$1 billion	26	$31.18
Contracts ≥$500 million & <$1 billion	56	$39.59
Contracts ≥$250 million & <$500 million	59	$19.90
Contracts ≥$50 million & <$250 million	290	$29.54
Contracts <$50 million	1094	$18.44
Total, all contracts	1,525	$138.65
Deals over $50 million	431	$120.21
% of deals over $50 million	28%	87%

Figure 1.1 Contract Summary for Big Deals Closed Globally from January to October 2008

term of the contract (for example, US$100 million in annual revenue contracted for ten years is a US$1 billion deal).

You will see that the big deal surrounding Big Deals is that they are truly the growth engine for your firm to reach ultimate greatness. Globally, Big Deals represent nearly 90 percent of the total value of all new outsourcing deals contracted annually, while the number of Big Deals represents only about 30 percent of all deals awarded (see Figure 1.1).[9]

When our former employer, Satyam, started the Strategic Deals Group (SDG) in 2005–06, the chairman lobbed a minimum contract size for a Big Deal of US$250 million TCV onto the table. This amount was up for discussion when planning the goals and objectives for the coming year with a commensurate "target" for the organization to close a certain amount annually. Because the business units (BUs) had historically closed some Big Deals with several Fortune 500 companies to lay the foundation for Satyam's meteoric rise in revenues, the target did not seem unreasonable, at least to Satyam corporate. The view was, of course, different if you were responsible for sustaining the closure rate year after year. Using our best negotiation skills (often required more internally than externally), we pointed out that the industry was reporting, through analysts and advisers, that US$50 million TCV was a more appropriate definition for Big Deals. The name of the game was to leverage the company's investment in expert resources to close

Big Deals. The definition for closing Big Deals ultimately came to be defined as "strategic deals": those with a US$50 million TCV and above, or a lower TCV if the BU leader deemed the pursuit strategic to his business. SDG became a partner of the BUs in pursuing those strategic deals.

Thinking big was always the theme when we targeted higher-value deals for their growth potential. However, a more important question became the center of discussion: Were these deals required for sustainable growth? Clearly, a revenue or top-line financial statement gets attention. However, is the capital required for the resources and time to pursue these types of deals justified? What if you don't win the pursuit? Then money is directly lost from earnings on the bottom line. Many emerging Indian information technology (IT) global players, who were riding the wave of strong offshoring, cast some doubt on the need to pursue large deals for growth. The formative years of "India Inc." (a colloquial term used by the global media to refer to the corporate sector of India), in the mid-2000s, illustrate that the India IT players were being rather coy with their public comments related to pursuing Big Deals. Here are two views about Big Deals from industry giants that were floating around in the market in those days:

- Infosys believed that mega deals were not necessary to grow at 30–35 percent in FY2007 (although they had started a large deals group as early as 2003).
- Cognizant preferred *hunting licenses* rather than large deals, where upfront investments may be required.

Here are a few responses to the ever-vigilant investor, focusing on margin dilution and risk, related to the big global sourcing company experiences with bigger and bigger deals:

- Tata Consultancy Services (TCS) believed that, on the Pearl Group deal (a mega deal then), even though they were establishing and stabilizing themselves, the margins were a little less when compared to their overall margins in other deals during the same initial stage. But as TCS improved the processes, they expected that the margin in the Pearl deal would become equivalent to the margins they were used to getting. TCS expected the margins in this deal to move up to company averages within 2.5 to 3 years with increasing offshore proportion.[10]

- The Infosys-led ABN AMRO deal, contracted in April 2005, was largely margin-neutral over the deal and was diluted initially. We believe the margin in that deal was low in the initial two to four quarters, until the knowledge transition was completed, but it should be almost at company average over the life of the deal.
- Wipro always expected pricing to be margin-neutral on a mega deal it signed with General Motors in February 2006, and with no unlikely impact on margins in the long run.

The general sense from these statements is that the pursuit of large deals was certainly a catalyst to accelerating revenue growth in these globally emerging firms. The case for expecting a higher revenue growth rate from the pursuit of Big Deals is borne out by companies growing at more than 35 percent, in spite of an absence of large deals in the past. On the other hand, pursuing large deals without a balance of smaller deals leaves companies exposed to the business variations of a few deals, as opposed to a better balanced portfolio of many customers. The industry was torn; are Big Deals important or not?

Are Big Deals Important?

Categorically: *yes*. Undoubtedly, if one aspires to build a dominant presence in any market, the opportunities surrounding large deals should be pretty obvious. It is equally important to understand the pitfalls in these deals, especially in the context of endeavoring to enhance margins and build sustainable revenues.

The possibility of recouping lower margins early in a Big Deal, with higher margins over the life of the deal, is a fundamental productivity expectation. But it also brings a risk to longer-term deals for the service provider. Clarity is needed, in terms of three critical factors:

1. The pace at which margins can be enhanced during the tenure of the deal.
2. The parameters that would enable margin enhancement with respect to utilization; a higher offshore presence of employees; pricing; a younger workforce; and sales, general, and administration (SG&A) reduction.

3. Assurance that future cost increases, such as wage inflation, will be absorbed without leading to a dip in margins over the life of the deal.

One final note on the finances of Big Deals: pick your game carefully. A comment about pass-through system integration deals will outline our reasoning for saying this.

Pass-through deals can be explained with a simple example. Suppose you sign a US$100 million deal in which SAP software costs US$90 million and your services revenue is US$10 million. The US$90 million is passing through, because SAP gets the revenue, although all of the US$100 million shows as the total deal size for your company. (For the purpose of this discussion, we shall assume that such deals refer to transactions wherein the pass-through component is 80–90 percent of the value of the deal.)

We do not generally recommend such deals when:

- The value added from such deals is limited.
- The pass-through, being nil or having a low-single-digit margin, means the overall margin would be rather unattractive with the impact of pulling down margins at the company level.
- Our experience with the equipment business is limited, and for a low margin we may be picking up significant risk from a performance perspective.
- There could be a mismatch of cash flows that could put additional pressure of recovery on us.
- The move will not enable any favorable response from the investment community, given that it is margin-diluted.
- The multi-national players—IBM, EDS, and CSC—are not too keen to pursue such deals with the same vigor as they did in the past, because of the abovementioned reasons.

However, our recommendation is that when you do choose to pursue Big Deals, do not forget what your drivers are and that you are in it to win a Big Deal. The story in Box 1.1 describes a real-life example.

The bottom line is that Big Deals are an effective strategy to accelerate growth. Large deals are important to both buyer and seller, although the impact of a particular deal is relative to the size of each player.

Box 1.1: When to Walk

Early in Hetzel's negotiating career, he was attempting to close negotiations on a deal with about US$100 million TCV. Hetzel was working for a service provider who wanted to win the deal badly. The service provider was used to getting Big Deals.

During the course of the negotiation, the client became more and more inflexible on issues that Hetzel, typically, would not concede on, even with very large clients. Hetzel recommended his company no longer pursue this strategic deal. The business unit leaders chose to walk away from it, on the basis of Hetzel's recommendation.

The customer called back after a few days and wanted to start re-negotiating again, with a more win-win attitude. Eventually, the deal was successfully closed and delivered by Hetzel's organization.

The moral of the story is never to close a bad deal. The lesson: never underestimate the time and effort to close a deal. *All* deals are Big Deals in their importance to those involved in the closing.

Global Economics and IT Services: The Established vs. the Challengers

Legend has it that the term *offshoring* was coined by IBM during one of its large outsourcing deal pursuits at Kodak. We will leave it to the historians to analyze exactly when outsourcing and offshoring of IT began. What we do know for sure is that Ross Perot founded EDS in the 1960s and made a big splash by receiving lucrative Big Deal contracts from the U.S. government computerizing Medicare records. EDS went public in 1968, and the stock price shot up from US$16 a share to US$160 within days. *Fortune* magazine called Perot the "fastest, richest Texan" in a 1968 cover story.[11]

Similarly, CSC spun up into megaspace in the early 1970s, by transitioning the entire IT shop of General Dynamics. IBM Global Services transformed its existing operations to focus on services, as did Hewlett-Packard and Accenture (a spinoff from Arthur Andersen's consulting practice). However, one thing became very clear on the world stage in the 1970s and 1980s: India had quietly and methodically spawned a services industry of IT professionals, graduating thousands of IT software engineers annually from its great universities and selling their skills internationally.

The journalist and author Thomas Friedman made sense of the modern trends in globalization in his bestselling book *The World Is Flat*. A "flat world" to us means the ability to deliver products or services for our customers by leveraging the best talents and resources from all over the world at an appropriate price.

As simple economies become more complex and multiple steps are required to provide your products or services, "specialties" and "commodities" are introduced. Providing a specialty commands a premium from the buyer, but as specialties become commodities, the opportunity arises to "make or buy" each step, to achieve the ultimate quality, price and utility for your customer.

Before the flat world emerged, the make-or-buy decision was simply a domestic issue, meaning your neighbor would typically make the car component you would later buy inside his factory. Post-flat world, another neighbor a few streets down who runs his own tool shop makes the same item for less as a supplier or subcontractor to the factory. He has learned the specialty skills, along with many others, of producing a sub-element of the car at a lower cost than the factory, therefore making it more of a commodity. This commodity is made available to the factory to buy and assemble or integrate into the final car at a lower price.

When all is said and done, optimization of this supply-chain cycle is called productivity. It spurs on innovation and allows the global standard of living to rise. However, with nations such as India, China, Brazil, and Russia emerging as economic powers, it may also prompt economic challenges between nations; standards of living cause work content to move around the world to achieve that ultimate supply-chain value for the global consumer. Yesterday, only major corporations were worried about global sourcing, international procurement, and foreign offsets. Today, with freedom of movement and lower-cost global supply chains, even a local automotive parts maker is likely to buy some products globally or, in the worst case, buy nothing and be completely replaced by the cheaper provider.

The maturity of any industry is a function of its constant metamorphosis into a more efficient, creative delivery system for its consumers. You need not look too far back in history to validate this message. The manufacturing industry in North America, and in particular the automotive industry, was forced into this game as Japan emerged on the global stage after World War II.

This introduction of free exchange of assets caused another phenomenon in the early days of manufacturing, known as make-versus-buy. Do you send a requisition to your purchasing department to buy subcomponents, or do you buy only the raw materials and use your own resources to make them? As long as businesses are growing and the make-versus-buy process does not upset the human-capital equation (translation: job losses), then it is a pure capital competition to provide the best value at the lowest total cost.

The companies that are likely to dominate their industries tomorrow will have global customers, global investors, global suppliers, global employees, and truly global societal responsibilities. Will today's American car manufacturers—General Motors, Ford, Chrysler—survive the challenges posed by Toyota, Honda, Hyundai, or Tata from India? During publication of this book, Tata was in the process of creating the world's cheapest car, the Nano. Similarly, the traditional big six IT service providers—IBM Global Services, Accenture, EDS, HP, CSC, and Capgemini (and in Europe Atos Origin)—face serious challenges from the India Inc. players. Today, TCS, Wipro, HCL, and Cognizant (together making up India Inc., for all practical purposes) all have more than US$2 billion in revenue and are poised to ceaselessly threaten the old and the established. As the world shrinks into Friedman's flat world, who will dominate or merely survive in their industry will be determined by who demonstrates the most efficient use of capital and resources to delight customers, no matter where they are in the world.

For companies to win deals today, simply delivering a product or service at a lower price point than the competitor's is not enough. Service providers need to come up with their own methodologies on how they will create differentiators.

How Will This Book Help You Win Big Deals?

This book will help you achieve two things:

1. *Understand the entire Big Deal life cycle* We will show you all the stages involved, from an insiders' view—both buyer and seller—because we have experienced both sides of the deal equation. We do not know of another book, at the time of publishing, that walks you through the entire gamut.

2. *Apply deal-proven best practices for each Big Deal stage* We will share with you our knowledge of the actual, applicable best practices (not academic or research-based but grounded in experience) needed in each stage of the deal life cycle. We will also give you the foundation needed to apply some of these lessons in your own environment.

That said, it would be ridiculous to claim that reading a book on winning deals can guarantee you will win them. But we can say with certainty that by following the principles explored in this book your probability of increasing your overall win rate should improve.

Winning a big global sourcing services deal is an all-round team effort involving the deals team, the vertical and horizontal business units, the account team, and the delivery organization. Getting a complete grasp of how the entire ecosystem works will definitely improve your chances of winning Big Deals.

But before you embark on the journey of winning deals, you should invest in doing a thorough bid analysis to properly assess the winning probability for a deal. Historically, we have seen many providers ignore the bid-no-bid analysis and jump straight into bidding. A thorough understanding of the processes involved will help you craft the right strategy to win the Big Deals—or at least give you sufficient reason to walk away from pursuing one.

Three groups of stakeholders are involved in pursuit and closure of any Big Deal, and all three are critical to its success. A decision to bid or not bid on a Big Deal should center on understanding the values that we as service providers bring to the group, individually and as a whole. The three stakeholders are:

1. The customer—the buyer or outsourcer of the services.
2. The service provider—you, the supplier of the outsourced work.
3. The influencers—client consultants and outside legal consultants, such as Jones Day, Mayer Brown, and Shaw Pittman (now part of Pillsbury Law), and third-party advisors (for example, Technology Partners, EquaTerra, and Everest). It also includes the competition in the pursuit.

A quick review of these three categories can give you a litmus test and help you decide whether to pursue or not pursue a Big Deal, or highlight your weaknesses in that particular endeavor.

Customer factors The big question in this category is to analyze if the customer will make an award. Will they ultimately sign on the dotted line? Will they really outsource the business? The most formidable competitor in many deals is the "no award" decision. This is always a customer option, though often not stated. We recommend that every provider go through a series of simple questions to score a probability of commitment on behalf of the customer. Scoring these questions from 1 to 5, with 5 being high commitment, is one way to understand the customer's commitment to the sell.

Service provider (supplier) factors Service providers should examine the evaluation factors in Figure 1.2, which, if honestly considered, will show your team's weaknesses or areas for improvement.

Influencer factors For the influencer category, we recommend that you keep it simple. For every influencer involved in the deal, rather than score factors numerically, a simple assessment of positive, negative, or neutral will give the pursuit team adequate information to evaluate the ability to close the deal. Figure 1.2 is a pictorial view of this litmus test.

A Review of Critical Success Factors
(1–5 Rating Scale Representing Low to High)

Customer Factors		**Service Provider Factors**	
1	Executive commitment	1	Executive sponsor
2	Clear strategy and objectives	2	Dedicated cross-functional team
3	Structured decision process	3	Onsite presence throughout process
4	Defined retained resources	4	Integrated roles and responsibilities
5	Accountability for results	5	Creative solutions
		6	Winning attitude

Total rating at max = 25 Total rating at max = 30
If rating <20 then do not bid If rating <24 then do not bid

Influencers
1 Competition
2 Third party advisors (TPAs)
   Is rating positive, neutral, or negative?

Figure 1.2 A Litmus Test to Evaluate Chances of Winning a Big Deal

Conclusion

Throughout this book, we have not shied away from borrowing best practices from non-industry people who we think can add value to the global sourcing industry. One such interesting individual we talked to was tennis star and entrepreneur, Mahesh Bhupathi, from India. Mahesh is an 11-time doubles Grand Slam winner, and the former world number one doubles player, but more importantly he may be the only active professional athlete on the planet who manages a multi-million-dollar business, hands on, while playing full-time tennis. His company, Globosport, is involved in brand consultancy, film production, and managing everything from movie stars and events to top athletes. When asked how he manages to get a Who's Who list of clients onto his roster and build his business so rapidly while handling an exceptionally busy travel schedule, he answered: "By building relationships at the executive level."

As you go through this book, you will find the overarching theme of building relationships. If you take away just one item from this book, we hope you will remember "Relationships matter!" As Mahesh has shown us, a lack of time need not be an excuse for not building relationships. We do have a word of caution about relationships, though. Simply building relationships without delivering appropriately is of no use. It is up to you, as a deal maker, to ensure that your delivery teams actually do the promised work. As Mahesh mentions, building relationships but not being dependable and reliable in delivery will actually backfire more than having no relationship at all.

In the following chapters, we lay out a very simple methodology for increasing the probability of closing any Big Deal. How you make use of the knowledge we present will significantly affect the win rate of your new business.

Notes

1. See http://www.csc.com/newsandevents/news/737.shtml.
2. See www.csc.com/newsandevents/news/1359.shtml.
3. See www.csc.com/newsandevents/news/2045.shtml.
4. See www.csc.com/investor_relations/press_releases/1167.
5. See www.csc.com/newsandevents/news/3077.shtml.
6. See http://www.dnaindia.com/report.asp?NewsID=1013197&CatID=4.
7. See http://qantas-news.newslib.com/story/7978-1513/.

8. See http://www.satyam.com/media/pr3oct07.asp.
9. For further information see http://www.datamonitor.com/ (January to October 2008).
10. On the Pearl Group deal: This £486 million deal (nearly US$1 billion), executable over twelve years, will consolidate thirteen systems (twelve homegrown and one from CSC) to Integrated Insurance Management Systems (IIMS). Pearl's 950 employees will move to Diligenta, the joint-venture company set up to execute the deal in which TCS holds 75 percent and Pearl holds the balance. Plans for this deal was announced in October 2005, and the transaction closed in April 2006.
11. See http://en.wikipedia.org/wiki/Ross_Perot, May 27, 2009.

CHAPTER 2

Getting the Right People Ready to Win Large Deals

Introducing Some Essential Concepts of the Human Element of Management

Most novice deal makers think that deals are won or lost because of the virtues of a few core team members who can swing the outcome of the deal one way or the other. Hollywood has done its part in promoting the individual heroism of deal makers as well. One can never forget the legendary independent film from 1992, *Glengarry Glen Ross,*[1] where Ricky Roma, played by Al Pacino, is a smooth-talking, questionably ethical deal maker who possesses an unhealthy killer instinct. By the end of the movie, either you want to be Ricky or you hate everything about him.

Although the deal-making phenomenon portrayed in the film looks suave and maybe even heroic, it does not necessarily depict reality. Deals are won—and, most important, delivered well—when the whole organization works in sync. Deal makers in the technology-sourcing industry have to find synergy with sales, delivery, and alliance teams, multiple-domain and competency-based business units, and support groups to win and deliver large deals.

The service providers, which are companies such as IBM, CSC, and Infosys from India Inc, are also successful because of their global delivery models. A service provider, with its people in multiple locations around the world, is always expected to work in sync as a human supply chain to deliver superior results for the client. In 90 percent of cases, these people never even meet each other face to face. This distributed-delivery model of pursuing and working deals results in a lot of human resource challenges. We believe that many organizations fail to deliver the intended results in large deals because they face two distinct human resource challenges: *operational* and *emotional.*

Companies have long looked at improving processes, quality, and the like to reduce the operational challenges involving people. Among these challenges are unnecessary duplication of effort, lost opportunities because of mismanagement, pursuing strategies that result in diseconomies of scale, overlapping roles, and lack of technical or functional competency. There are many fantastic books on the market that focus on how to streamline operations in order to do business better. But our combined experience, working for India Inc. as well as Fortune 500 companies, has taught us that the emotional elements of the human resource challenge are harder to fix. If you have ever been in a relationship with a loved one in personal life, you know this all too well. We hope that by the end of this chapter you will have a good understanding of the human aspect of emotional challenges and be able to take appropriate measures to counter them.

Analyzing Emotional Challenges: A Hard Look at Large Deals

Emotional Intelligence Quotient, or EQ, is the model promoted by Daniel Goleman in his 1995 book *Emotional Intelligence.*[2] Although many believe that the role of the Intelligence Quotient (IQ), or inherited competency, is extremely valuable when hiring employees, EQ is often given less weight. EQ permits a new insight in understanding the "feelings" part of the human equation. We believe that to win large deals, where the whole organization is mobilized, management needs to address emotional issues first. Our goal is to present to you some real-life scenarios that resulted in deep emotional scars, ultimately hurting the deal (see Box 2.1).

The story depicted in the box is not unique, and clearly the provider factors that rated low were people issues. During preparation for this book, we talked to deal leaders who shepherd large deals in multinationals, such as CSC, IBM, Accenture, Capgemini, and Deloitte; and India Inc. leaders, such as Infosys, Wipro, and Tata Consultancy Services (TCS). Interestingly enough, we found that the major common issues, with respect to getting the deal team mobilized during the pursuit or delivery processes, can be divided into two distinct issues: (1) challenges as seen through the eyes of management, and (2) challenges as seen through the eyes of employees.

Box 2.1: When People Go Astray: A Tale of the Human Supply Chain*

We were both part of a very large global pursuit in the early part of 2007 when we were working for a major Indian service provider. Hetzel was involved to oversee the pursuit-process deployment and offer suggestions to the business unit leader. Anirban was the deal director; his role was to own the problem statement of the customer, working together with our company's BU champion. Together, the Strategic Deals Group (SDG) deal director and BU champion were responsible for taking all necessary measures to iron out problems by assembling the right brains from various parts of the company. These people would then work uniformly to create the proposal response for the customer.

It was a classic case of global supply-chain management applied to a bidding process. The customer was a global industry leader, headquartered in Europe, with penetration in almost all parts of the world. The core proposal pursuit team, including Anirban, was operating out of London with its members shuttling between multiple cities in Europe while constantly networking with the customer. The competency delivery unit teams, such as the SAP team and the application development team, were operating out of India; the executive team, representing multiple business units, was chiming in from all over the globe. Several deal-team members from SDG were supporting the bid from Europe. Finally, other teams, such as finance and HR, were working on the deal from corporate headquarters in India.

The work breakdown structure (WBS) was laid out early in the game, the core team was identified, and the common goal and win themes were acknowledged and understood. The bid duration was about six months. For the first two weeks, everything worked well. Two weeks into the deal, the mechanism started falling apart. A lot of the people who were supposed to offer input for the proposal were being put onto other assignments by their immediate supervisors. Although the deal director was well identified, there was no clear, defined line of authority. People started missing deadlines, the solution definition was not

(*continued*)

coming along properly, and time was simply flying by with very little progress. Executive escalations were rampant, but the escalated issues got lost in a blame game.

The bid was eventually submitted successfully. However, the ultimate result was a loss. In retrospect, if we had taken a look at the win-loss principles in Chapter One of this book, we could have predicted our failure. As you will recall, there are three factors for consideration of win-loss success: customers, service providers, and influencers. The customer factor scored 21, which showed they were highly likely to select a provider. But our company's probability-to-win rating was 19, which showed we probably should not have bid in the first place. Figures 2.1 and 2.2 depict the actual bid-no-bid analysis for this pursuit.

[*] We have changed some of the details of this anecdote so as not to disclose the specific pursuit, but the learning portrayed is still paramount.

Challenges as Seen Through the Eyes of Management

Senior managers of any organization typically have a different point of view on just about anything compared to the regular employee base. This is mainly because senior management tends to be macro-focused, whereas the rank and file are focused on a micro-level outcome. When it comes to playing pop psychologist and evaluating emotional

Critical Success Factors
(1–5 Rating Scale Representing Low to High)

Customer Factors	Example Ratings
1 Executive commitment	1 CXO alignment: 5
2 Clear strategy and objectives	2 Goals and objectives stated: 4
3 Structured decision process	3 Hired third-party advisor (TPA): 4
4 Clearly defined scope	4 Defined retained resources: 3
5 Compelling events	5 Accountability for results: 5
	6 Winning attitude: 4

**25 out of 30 = 83.3%; this customer is
likely to make an award**

Figure 2.1 Critical Success Factors (Customer)

Supplier Factors of Win Vs. Loss (1–5 Rating Scale Representing Low to High)	
Supplier Factors	**Service Provider Ratings**
1 Executive sponsor	1 BU commitment: 3
2 Cross-functional team	2 Cross-functional team: 3
3 Good onsite presence	3 Onsite PMO: 4
4 Defined roles	4 Defined roles: 3
5 Creative solution	5 Successful reviews: 3
6 Winning attitude	6 Winning attitude: 3
	19 out of 30 = 63%; this service provider should not bid

Figure 2.2 Critical Success Factors (Provider)

challenges of team members, we found that management views also differ considerably from those of employees.

Lack of Interest

One of the most common problems that deal teams face in mobilizing the extended team is that many team members do not assume ownership of their tasks. They may be doing exactly what they are expected to do as per the work breakdown structure (WBS), but they never go the extra mile in making sure that the company wins the deal. It is a common challenge for deal directors to energize the entire team to see beyond the task level and take action above and beyond the call of duty. This phenomenon is clearly manifested in proposal responses. Once, a few years back, a reputable analyst invited Anirban to a meeting. He displayed parts of a proposal response for the same bid from four service providers. Three of those service providers were India Inc. members, and one was a global system integrator. The proposals were shown on the screen, side by side, hiding the names of the service providers and the customer. Essentially, the question asked was, What would the service provider do to govern the existing processes for the customer? Three of the four service providers wrote virtually identical answers describing the virtues of the project management practices in their respective companies. The answers were not especially customized, and it looked as though they were all copied and pasted from the same playbook. This is a perfect example of lack of ownership. Basically, the people responding to the question did their job by answering the question, but without really taking the time to do so in a desired contextual form. Just one service provider of the four actually took time to read the question, analyze it thoroughly, and respond accordingly.

The Gunslinger's Attitude

The solution response to a proposal or solution delivery for a large deal is never straightforward. One can provide a solution for the customer in many ways. Typically, the solution team goes through a rigorous exercise to come up with the best possible solution scenario. However, there are always a few employees, mainly from technology units, who document their own ideas in the proposal response, in variance to what has really been agreed on as a group. These are the gunslingers, folks who are ready to shoot at the drop of a dime. Sometimes the situation gets even worse when these gunslingers start communicating directly with the customer, or the third-party advisor (TPA) assisting the customer. Their selling agenda (camouflaged as communication) often jeopardizes the sanctity of the deal. Although less prevalent now because of greater dependence on standardized procedures, gun-slingers in delivery units also tend to do work outside their presumed scope because they believe it is beneficial for the customer. This effort is called "gold plating" and is an absolute no-no. Although the gold-plating intention is good, non-contracted work outside the defined service level agreement (SLA) opens up opportunities for the customer to get the upper hand if the new work somehow damages the end product. Gold plating can be a costly mistake for the service provider. In short, beware of people who are unpredictable in how they operate from an organization resource management standpoint.

Defensive Passion

Because deal teams are so globally distributed and have representatives from multiple cultures, it is often very easy to step on others' toes unknowingly. We have worked with several exceptionally bright finan-cial leaders who are well educated and very knowledgeable about accounting principles. But if questioned on any of the assumptions they propagate, they often tend to get furious. The vigorous defense generally comes from this angle: "We've done this hundreds of times;

how dare you challenge the call?" At the other end of the spectrum, there may be people on the deals team with certain solution-providing responsibilities who are not quite the experts they should be. When challenged, they tend to go on the defensive to show they know their stuff. They do not want people questioning their capabilities (or lack of). Sometimes, on a much simpler level, people respond differently to questions during bid calls without realizing how their audience will receive it. The theme of the response, given from hundreds or thousands of miles away, is lost in translation, leaving the team with a negative impression. The point here is the pursuit team leader as well as every member on the team should push one another to be supportive and collaborative. If a team uses up its competitive energy internally, rest assured the best solutions will not be passed on to your customers.

Challenges as Seen Through the Eyes of Employees

But it's not just management that feels the human resource challenges during the deals process. The employees have their own challenges. The next few paragraphs define these challenges through the eyes of the people who actually have boots on the ground, the people writing the response, doing the coding, and basically keeping the lights on.

Feeling Used and Abused

When we talked to bid-team members of large deals across many organizations, we found that the most common complaint is that management does not keep employees in the loop. In fact, the people who are actually doing the work are often purposely kept outside the loop. This sends a strong message of lack of trust.

Let's discuss this by way of the real-life example in Box 2.2.

Let's step back again and do a post mortem on the win-loss factors in this vignette. Again, the customer was committed, scoring 22 out of 25. The provider factors this time around were much higher—26 out of 30—primarily because management commitment was high and the team was small and dedicated.

So, does the end justify the means? Are there long-term repercussions if employees do not feel included? Are there better ways to handle bid-team management?

We believe that deal-makers and BU leaders need to be highly cognizant of this human aspect of inclusion if they are to groom the

Box 2.2: The Unintended Repercussions of Need-to-Know Policies

In the middle of 2008, our company had the opportunity to offer an indicative proposal to a major high-tech customer. Basically, the customer wanted us to put together a proposal to acquire part of their business in Asia. Because employee acquisition was part of the package, this proposal was highly sensitive in nature. The customer did not want to broadcast the news to its employees and shareholders because of potential repercussions from those quarters. So the vertical business unit championing this deal wanted to keep a lid on it. They were well justified in doing so.

A deal team was formed with core and extended team members. They were all briefed about the sensitivity of this deal and how important it was for everyone to win it and act as one team. A junior bid manager was assigned to manage daily calls, WBS, and responses. She also tried her best to have regular communication with the entire team, educating them about the bid progress.

People were working hard responding to the proposal and getting ready to defend it in front of the customer. For a while, everybody felt a sense of ownership. However, somewhere along the way, senior management involved in the deal started having need-to-know discussions with several members of the team on specific topics such as pricing, legal, and strategy. Very soon, multiple need-to-know meetings were going on simultaneously at every pay-grade level among deal-team members. Sometimes, these discussions were on the same topics, causing duplication of effort. The rest of the team, who were not invited to these meetings, were also kept in the dark about new developments transpiring from the discussions. In addition, the people who were sought after as part of these meetings were left high and dry once they finished giving their feedback in those sessions. The net result was that what was briefed as part of the deal communication to the entire team was not actually happening on the ground.

Although secrecy was instigated by design and by accident, either way it sapped the morale of the team, especially in the lower rungs. People constantly complained of not feeling included. On the flip side, the end result was great. We managed to beat the competitors and ended up winning the deal.

next generation of leaders to take over when needed. Besides, if done badly, this can also affect morale to the point where employees become vengeful against the organization as a whole.

Feeling Unnecessarily Scrutinized

These days, deal teams are so dispersed among many locations that it is almost impossible to manage these teams by walking around. Deal directors have to rely on electronic means of communication to keep tabs on the progress of the group. It is not uncommon for plans to be laid out but not followed because some team members (remember the gunslingers from earlier?) do not believe in the leadership. Many deal-makers constantly probe the work of the team, contacting team members at all hours to ensure that work is done. This constant monitoring makes the junior team members feel they are being un-necessarily scrutinized or micro-managed.

Mitigating Emotional Challenges, Solution One: Modify Management Behavior

In discussing a cure for these challenges, we found that people were providing us with very detailed management theories. These theories are great, but we were really seeking real-life lessons grounded in reality. Our answers came from Balu T., who heads service delivery for our company's telecom infrastructure group. Balu has many years of experience managing globally distributed teams. But more important, he is quite a philosopher and likes to dive into analyzing human behavior and study group dynamics for fun. Anybody who knows Balu can attest to his dramatic, sometimes profanity-laden way of explaining things, in terms people generally do not forget. Who better to ask, to get some candid feedback on this topic?

Interestingly enough, Balu referred us to a paper he wrote on this very subject, called "Trains and Rockets: An Essay on Leaders and Leader-ship."[3] This paper captures three main tenets for managing HR chal-lenges related to emotional and cultural issues in large-deal bid teams:

1. Creating a defined sense of purpose: "What am I doing here?"
2. What is the direction? "What are my steps to my goal? What is my job?"
3. Maintaining team morale: "Can a cookie-cutter approach work?"

Tenet One: Creating a Defined Sense of Purpose: "What Am I Doing Here?"

It does not take a rocket scientist to understand that thinking leads to strategy. Simply speaking, thinking is a roadmap for solving problems. But it is the EQ that drives people to act on implementing strategy. It is the leader's role to create a sense of purpose the whole team identifies with. For example, let us look at the luxury hotel chain Four Seasons. Its core differentiator is service, not just what it offers as amenities. Every employee, from the dishwasher to the resort manager, identifies with the mission of making the customer feel special. Employees go out of their way to do things for guests because the philosophy of providing unparalleled service is ingrained in the DNA of the company. An example of this common purpose was when a housekeeper from the Dallas Four Seasons drove a hotel guest to a special *ayurvedic* spa on the employee's day off. This was not done for a tip, but simply because the guest said she wished she were able to go to such a spa.

Balu identifies Mohandas Karamchand Gandhi as an example of a leader who can impart a clear direction and set an understandable purpose. Despite all of India saying it would be impossible to lay down arms at a time when nationalist sentiments were igniting fire in people's hearts, Gandhi was successful in persuading people to adopt a non-violent way of protesting. Historians may differ in how successful Gandhi was in achieving his intention through purely non-violent means. There were many other leaders in the India of the time, among them Netaji Subhas Chandra Bose, who championed a "blood for blood" *mantra* in fighting the colonial power of the British. He even solicited help from Adolf Hitler to defeat them. But regardless of how successful Gandhi's efforts were, his message of non-violence became a worldwide phenomenon. Gandhi has since become an icon representing the principle of non-violence.

During the 2008 U.S. election campaign season, Barack Obama was almost as popular as a rock star. Although some people may have questioned his experience to run for the presidency, his inspirational speeches, calculated political moves, calls for change, and star quality got millions of Americans excited about the voting process. Obama the enigma may have been a main reason for the landslide victory in favor of the Democrats, a victory that almost crippled the Republican party. Anyone who followed the 2008 presidential campaign can attest to the fact that he has been able to revitalize the Democratic

Party once again and bring in people to join his cause from the center and the right.

A deal leader can find a lot of commonality among the Four Seasons, Gandhi, and Obama. All were able to excite their stakeholders into believing in a common cause. We believe that if this tenet is implemented correctly, it will help eradicate (or at least reduce) some of the EQ challenges such as employees lacking interest, or feeling used and abused. We also believe that this strategy of setting a clear purpose will help turn defensive passions into energetic, enthusiastic ones.

Tenet Two: What Is the Direction? "What Are My Steps to My Goal? What Is My Job?"

Typically, large organizations have the capability to win and deliver large deals. However, large organizations can also be rigid in nature. In the preceding box, we described how intentionally, or unintentionally, deal teams start losing transparency. Although WBSs are created and timelines for deliverables are established, lack of open communication creates several negative aspects, notably the energizing of negative, defensive gunslingers.

Our experience has taught us that use of hidden need-to-know meetings and sidebar conversations should be kept to a minimum. These activities definitely damage team dynamics. Transparency will force deal managers to be fair to all, reducing employee anxiety about being unfairly criticized.

Balu T. describes this phenomenon ingeniously in his paper. He gives the example of a train and a rocket as leadership styles. A train has a leader in the form of an engine and a "team" of carriages that follow the direction of the leader. The goal is not to leave any carriages behind. In contrast, a rocket is more non-collaborative. If you look at how rockets are launched, each stage is there to set the groundwork for the next stage. Once this has been accomplished, the stage is disposed of. Although the goal is achieved, it is not an all-inclusive and collaborative approach.

We are definitely proponents of Balu's train approach for leading teams. All status and tasks are treated as equal from a moral perspective, even where a task hierarchy exists. So, regardless of whether one is leading the pursuit as a deal director, or simply furnishing man-hours for SAP delivery work, both are equal in the social hierarchy. This helps clarify direction and ensures people know what to expect.

Tenet Three: Maintaining Team Morale: "Can a Cookie-Cutter Approach Work?"

Whenever bids are in progress for a long period of time, it is very important for the bid leaders to constantly assess the morale of the team and take appropriate action. For instance, it is the duty of the deal leaders to take stern action against gunslingers, continuous naysayers, and those who are simply not interested. However, it is extremely important that leaders not only focus on the end results but also look at the causes of disaffection. Should the disinterested person—perhaps going through a bitter divorce and custody battle—be treated the same as a person who just wants to surf the Web rather than work? Do you treat them differently although their end results are the same? We believe leaders need to show extra initiative to explore the human emotions involved rather than simply look at HR issues from a policy standpoint. We believe that as a deal navigator you will see positive results out of the team if you maintain transparency, recognize achievements, and conduct collaborative and inclusive leadership. Above all, adopt a human approach with the team.

Mitigating Emotional Challenges, Solution Two: It's All About Talent Management

Our quest to find a broader cure to the HR problems of deal teams has taken us to Lori Blackman. Lori is the CEO of DNL Global, a Dallas-based talent management firm. DNL Global specializes in helping buyers and sellers find global sourcing experts at the executive level to fill their leadership void. When we interviewed Lori, we initially wanted to discuss how to build a deal team that would have the best chance to win business. What we understood from her was that a deal team cannot achieve great success if it does not fit into the broader organizational culture of the company. This makes sense; deal teams have to interact with almost every part of the organization to win and deliver large deals. So it is important to get the right talent at all levels, as opposed to simply putting together a deal team. We have all seen talented employees put into the wrong role or the wrong team. If the wrong person is part of a deal team, it can directly affect the stock price. It is extremely important for a supplier organization to view strategic hiring differently if it wants to continue winning large deals in the future.

Lori has been instrumental in working with the International Association of Outsourcing Professionals (IAOP) to champion the concept of Talent Portfolio Management for global sourcing. Talent Portfolio Management helps identify the right talent and put them in the proper role within an organization at the right time. Although this concept is not new, traditionally technology services organizations have primarily viewed resources from a competency-match perspective. For example, managers would look at a resume and ask, "Is this Java developer qualified to write code for us for this given requirement?" Talent Portfolio Management is a very different way to view a candidate. It asks, "How much value will this individual provide our organization based on these one hundred criteria, including emotional compatibility? The ability to develop Java-based code may be one criterion among them." The second approach is more holistic in nature and looks beyond identified roles in hiring candidates.

The simplest way to understand the concept of Talent Portfolio Management is to view talent like equities in a financial portfolio. Financial planners advise customers to assemble their equity portfolio according to criteria such as risk propensity, industry diversity, cost of equity, and global presence. Talent Portfolio Management uses the same logic of applying multiple and diverse criteria, coupled with a weighted average, to hiring resources. According to Lori Blackman:

> Talent Portfolio Management involves deciding what resources to include in a portfolio, given the goals of the business and the changing economic conditions. Selection involves deciding what resources to acquire, how many resources to acquire, under what terms, when to acquire each, and what resources to divest.[4]

We asked Lori a simple question: How is this hiring process any different from getting a candidate who passes a "behavioral interview"? Her answer was simple. The traditional behavioral interview focuses on a few dimensions of behavior and declares whether or not a person is a cultural fit. In most cases, what it does not do is:

- *Detailed assessment* Assess the person on the basis of technical, domain, functional, emotional, and behavioral aspects to find how he or she fits into the entire organization. Lori proposes using a very detailed evaluation as opposed to a general one.
- *Continuous assessment* Continuously assess the whole organization to shift people around, according to these criteria.

- *Hire not for role* View an incoming resource as a talent that fits the company rather than a particular role. Hiring managers need to think of talent as equities that are prescribed for a financial portfolio with a view to long-term financial goals. This is exactly the opposite of a trader's mentality, which looks for short-term gain by buying and selling stocks. Talents should be a long hold.

We believe that although technical and domain-based skills remain important in hiring decisions, organizations need to start assessing their organization culture and hiring people who fit that profile. HR departments, with the help of executive recruiting firms specializing in Talent Portfolio Management, need to address the issue of total compatibility fit rather than just requirement fit.

Conclusion: Two Ways to Increase the Probability of Success

We have suggested two ways to solve the emotional problems that may affect team dynamics. We believe leaders need to follow the behavioral approaches described here in order to mobilize their teams. In tandem, the HR process has to support the organization by hiring the right individual, one who fits not only professionally but also emotionally and culturally within the broad corporate culture. To win large deals consistently and continue delivering them successfully, one needs to be better at both modifying behavior and managing talent holistically. Managing these issues as part of the assessment of win-loss factors increases the probability of success.

Notes

1. See http://en.wikipedia.org/wiki/Glengarry_Glen_Ross_(film).
2. Daniel Goleman, *Emotional Intelligence: Why It Can Matter More Than IQ* (New York: Bantam, 1995).
3. Balu T. "Trains and Rockets: An Essay on Leaders and Leadership."
4. Adapted from discussions at the International Association of Outsourcing Professionals (IAOP) Global Human Capital Chapter Meeting, Sept. 18, 2008. http://www.outsourcingprofessional.org/content/23/162/1552/.

FINDING DEALS

CHAPTER 3

Finding Big Deals

Strategies to Discover High-Value Deals

If you do a survey among account managers, relationship managers, client partners, and business development executives and ask them a simple question—"Why is your Big Deals pipeline so dry?"—we guarantee you will get variations of the same answer: "It's very hard to find Big Deals." Account managers, relationship managers, and client partners have differing job titles, but they all share the same pain and challenges of serving and growing business within targeted accounts. For the purpose of this chapter, we use these job titles interchangeably. Business development executives also share the same growth challenges; however, they tend to trawl a broader geography to meet their revenue target.

The truth is that the global sourcing industry does not support a plethora of Big Deals. But Big Deals do happen. And because the number of Big Deals is far fewer than small or medium ones, it is important that as a provider you get to know about these deals long before they are awarded. Our goal in this chapter is to highlight some ways to help you find those deals.

Where Are Big Deals?

New business development executives need to focus on a few specific areas with potential to get new, sizeable business. Randomly cold-calling large corporations is a waste of time, at least in most cases. Here are two sources that can help new business developers build a solid base of sizeable deals: TPA (third-party advisors) and finding customers from the ground up.

TPAs (Third-Party Advisors)

This is probably the most sought-after business development channel among India Inc. players. TPAs are primarily power brokers that help craft a win-win scenario between the provider and the customer. Ideally, new business developers should explore this channel in collaboration with the company's TPA relationship manager. Because this channel requires significant attention, we dedicate the whole of Chapter Four to working with TPAs.

Finding Customers from the Ground Up

Such activity is the crux of new business development and the main focus of this chapter. A lot of frontline salespeople run around endlessly, hoping to get some Big Deals, without much success. What we have found is that because these salespeople are under tremendous pressure to make quarterly numbers, they are always in transactional mode and seldom venture into the unknown territory of strategically positioning themselves to scout for Big Deals.

Here, we demonstrate how salespeople can methodically win business from the ground up. We have identified two ways in which business development executives can find new large deals: finding deals by going after deal renewals, and penetrating and radiating (getting Big Deals within established business).

Finding Deals by Going After Deal Renewals

Companies specializing in business intelligence, such as Datamonitor,[1] produce a list of industry deal renewals broken down by customer name, industry, competency area, region, incumbent, deal size in revenue terms, and renewal date. These lists are great for business development leaders looking to initiate contact with a potential customer a year or two before the deal renewal date. If the relationship between the customer and the incumbent has gone sour or faces serious challenges that have an impact on business, it gives you (the potential new provider) a good starting point for discussion. Historically, these renewals are almost always continued with the same provider; however, in the last five years an increasing number have gone to new service providers. For a peek into how enormous the global renewal market is, take a look

Table 3-1 Global Deal Renewals Till 2012

Industry	Number of Deals Ending Between 4/1/09 and 3/31/12	Total Contract Value in US$ Billion
Banking	500	$43.12
Government	1,807	$148.97
Energy and utility	158	$10.63
Health care	214	$14.92
Insurance	214	$15.69
Logistics	14	$1.77
Manufacturing	445	$38.79
Media and entertainment	44	$0.75
Retail	175	$8.07
Services	492	$21.33
Technology	137	$10.10
Telecom	545	$62.02
Travel and transportation	239	$12.11
Others	76	$7.76

Source: Datamonitor.

at Table 3.1. Some 5,000 deals with a TCV of US$396 billion of sourcing work is up for renewal. Even if the incumbent gets the bulk of the work, does it not make sense to chase this pipeline even if a new provider can get only a fraction?

We have seen that salespeople often adopt the traditional method of engaging in dialogue at the middle-management level for way too long. Sometimes the discussion can last for many months. Although these customer sources are great to present an accurate picture of the sourcing relationship, project managers, program managers, or other middle-management personnel cannot usually make game-changing decisions on provider selection for large deals. Because the time to create an opportunity is short, it is critical that salespeople reach executive management decision makers as quickly as possible. At this point, building rapport from the ground up is not an option.

We advise that if you are planning to go after renewals, start as early as two years before the contract expires, and find a way to reach the customer executives. There are several companies, known as business associates, specializing in securing appointments with executives at target companies. Typically, in the U.S. these companies charge about US$500 to get you an appointment. You can also use your existing relationship with the customer's partners, customer's customers (you may have a relationship with them that can be leveraged), or any other sources to help you get there. The point is that the pitch about relieving top-line or bottom-line pain needs to be delivered at the topmost customer executive level and as early as possible.

Penetrate and Radiate: Getting Big Deals Within Established Business

This is probably the most common strategy for getting large deals, and we focus primarily on it in this chapter. This strategy assumes you are already established within an account, probably have some presence in parts of a company, and are now focused on growing the account. Although this type of account management strategy sounds simple to plan, it is tough to execute. Getting Big Deals within established accounts is truly a mix of science and art. The science part is the process and the art part is the soft skills required to execute it. Although every organization has its own processes and best practices, they are quite similar in nature.

But before you even think about uncovering large deals in existing accounts, you need to ensure that your company is already doing top-notch work. If you talk to the old warhorse Brent Davidson, he will tell you that doing existing work well is the most important step in getting Big Deals in existing accounts. He is a seasoned relationship manager with IBM who has succeeded in unearthing several Big Deals from the Fortune 100 customers he manages. Brent recommends three simple steps that work well with all accounts, and we recommend an adjunct to the third one.

1. *Rule one: Be honest about deliverables* Honesty about deliverables is probably the most important rule if you are seeking customer trust. You need to be comfortable with the fact that service delivery will have issues. Nobody expects completely issue-free operations. Your job as relationship manager is to ensure that you give the customer accurate status. Obviously, you need to be sensitive about the method of communication; you definitely do not want to announce problems using mass emails, for instance. However, if a major delivery is at jeopardy, the best way to handle it is to be

upfront with the customer and present a problem resolution plan. Simply being honest about the problem without showing how you are trying to fix it (even if the plan is not complete) is just not enough. Repeated honesty in disclosing problems and sincerity in trying to resolve them will help you turn customers into internal champions for you. These champions will pave the way for the next deal.

2. *Rule two: Don't harass your customer (or the TPA)!* Once you get a deal in an existing account, take some time to engage there. Relationship managers should focus on delivery rather than upfront sales. If delivery is done right, your contacts with your customer, who are reaping the benefits of your good delivery, will become the salespeople for you. Doing sales calls within a new account is great. But as a salesperson, the approach is to soft-pedal your way in and not push sales. Many inexperienced salespeople try too hard when the customer is not giving time. They increase the frequency of making sales calls, but the result is no deals, and definitely a customer who is annoyed (or worse). It is best to slowly build the relationship and then talk sales, not vice versa.

3. *Rule three: Relate on a personal level* Brent was the relationship manager for his customer, a major telecom provider, for many years. He eventually became one of the most loved relationship managers at this organization. He was invited by his customers to *bar mitzvahs* and fishing trips quite regularly. His secret for this level of relationship is to relate on a personal level. Brent ensured that he always got to know individuals personally outside their professional role.

Building Broad-Based Networks

A broad-based people network serves exactly the same purpose as a technical network: formation of a superior communication system. Connecting at a personal level puts you in touch with the core values of people who do business with people.

Building a broad-based network includes connecting with associates at work; with your local neighbors, family, and friends; and, of course, with professional associations. The point of these *relationships* is the *relate* part. It is easier to do business with those with whom you can relate. The personal connections here are critical because they promote trust and familiarity (see Box 3.1).

Box 3.1: Why Relationships Matter

Hetzel once pursued a major deal for more than 12 months. There were only two competitors left at the decision point, but the potential customer still could not pull the trigger and select one provider. As the two competitors continued to maneuver for a decision, executive management at Hetzel's company happened to attend a networking function where the TPA who had been working with this client was also present. These executives queried the TPA regarding the lack of progress in his client's decision making. The TPA executive said very simply, "Neither you nor your competition [both India-based firms] have developed a strong enough personal relationship with this client to make them comfortable at a personal level that you have their best interests at heart." His parting nugget: "You need to become a part of their neighborhoods, schools, and participate in shared recreational activities. Then, when they wake up in the middle of the night with a major work catastrophe, they will not hesitate to pick up the phone and call you."

We understand that the TPA executive's statement regarding becoming a part of every customer's neighborhood, school, and recreational circle may be rhetorical, but if the focus is indeed on building personal friendships, miracles happen. One caveat though: you cannot force customer friendship. You have to ease into it. Many times, provider executives from faraway countries expect that relationship managers will become customer buddies right away. That's a sure way to court disaster.

But account development also requires some specific skills beyond the best practices described here. To learn about some industry best practices from an account development teacher, we contacted Ted Ehling, the CEO of Balanced Performance. Ted helps client partners, relationship managers, and account managers from global sourcing service providers develop strategies to grow account penetration. Ted has also worked as a TPA and as a provider with EDS and Covansys. So he has experience from many vantage points. The next section summarizes what we heard from Ted as well as our experience of working with teams focused on account growth.

Account Development Strategy

The first step in an account development strategy is working closely with the customer to gain a basic understanding of their organizational structure. This is where you map your organizational capabilities onto the customer's organizational needs. To get a Big Deal in an existing account, it is extremely important to have a deep and broad relationship. Providers often build deep relationships in the area they work in. But for a large customer with wide geographical distribution, account penetration in silos won't help in spreading relationships at all levels. This means little chance of creating a Big Deal there. When we talk to relationship managers or account managers at various providers, the biggest complaint we hear is that they do not have the people to grow relationships outside their immediate business. Many times, it is because the relationship managers try to do it all by themselves. It is impossible to be an effective CEO (the relationship manager is essentially a CEO for the named account representing the provider), manage existing operations, and grow relationships at all levels all by yourself.

We have seen our share of account managers who are hesitant in bringing in support personnel. Their biggest fear in leveraging the broader organization is that they may be overshadowed. That happens sometimes. Our advice for business leaders is to create an environment where the broader team supporting the account manager or relationship manager should never feel as if they have overtake the account manager to demonstrate their value-adds. Support measurement metrics should be created in a completely non-competing way that pose no threat to the account manager's role. This type of non-competing metric is the ultimate *nirvana*, which may never happen in real life. But as business leaders we ought to try to offer as much warm and fuzzy feeling as possible to the account managers. On the flip side, account managers should remember that if they land a Big Deal because of an extended team, they will still get credit. Additionally, it's an opportunity to get a bigger piece of the commission pie. So it is in everybody's interest to encourage your account managers to use the "all hands on deck" approach when trying to grow accounts.

We recommend that relationship managers focus on creating relationship metrics and managing them. Relationship metrics constitute a detailed document that maps provider associates, whether they are part of your account team or not, with key individuals in your customer account. For large accounts, your company CEO (the actual provider CEO) should be maintaining a relationship with the customer CEO or at least the unit CEO (senior vice president), and your program managers should be managing a relationship with the customer program managers. We have seen good relationship managers extend this network even to the programmer level. Relationship managers should not hesitate in requesting the help of support teams, such as the deals group, who may have deal directors with prior sales experience. Good relationship managers are experts in ensuring that all these relationships are working well, so that the right messages are flowing in and out at all levels. The goal is to produce exceptional customer satisfaction.

The relationship manager should also ensure that the whole account team is working closely with the customer in doing project review, analysis, and forecasting and that there are discussions to create both short- and long-term actionable objectives. The objective here is to clearly identify significant customer pain points in multiple areas so that an indicative proposal can be put in place to address them. Here are four specific steps that account managers need to take in order to mine Big Deals:

1. Develop an understanding of the customer's lines of business (LOBs) across geographies.
2. Identify and match sourcing opportunities in areas of provider competency.
3. Identify potential roadblocks for sourcing, and plan a mitigation strategy.
4. Put indicative value proposition for sourcing in front of customer executives.

Although all these points are true and time-tested, nothing works if the relationship manager lacks clout internally. What happens when the relationship manager fails to influence the overseas delivery teams to deliver right? How can the relationship manager ensure that his boss's boss does not come in to do a hard sell to a sensitive customer? We strongly believe that if you are positioned as a relationship manager but have not been given the authority to influence decisions internally, you are being set up for failure. Customers also see this. In Box 3.2 is a real-life example of why clout matters.

Box 3.2: Why Clout Matters

Pioneer Natural Resources CIO Tom Halbouty told us an interesting story. Pioneer sourced some of their work to a UK-based service provider. The provider was an existing vendor for Pioneer, and their work was going great. Pioneer also did enough due diligence to ensure that this provider was entirely capable of doing top-notch work for this new work area.

After a few months of work, the Pioneer team grew extremely disappointed with the work. The provider missed deadlines, project overruns occurred, and customer satisfaction nosedived. Tom was shocked at the result because he knew that these guys know how to deliver.

Tom discovered that the problem was with a sub-contracted vendor. For this new work, the UK-based provider became the prime vendor and sub-contracted some of the work to a major India Inc. player. The sub-contractor was also very good but did not rise to the occasion in this case. On further investigation, Tom found that the work was hampered because the UK-based provider did not have enough clout with the India Inc. player (who was five times the size of the prime vendor) to get things done. So they always got the C team, as opposed to the A team, doing the work. The UK-based service provider's relationship manager at Pioneer was unable to influence his organization to put pressure on the sub-contractor to get things done right.

Eventually, the prime provider brought the work in-house and things improved dramatically.

The moral of the story is that relationship managers, account managers, and client partners need to be able to influence the organization to get things done, both internally and externally.

Sales Leadership Counts!

This chapter would be incomplete if we did not address sales leadership. It's no secret that whether you are in the business of selling shoes or high-end technology services, the salespeople in the field are the ones who bring the cash home. The senior executives, deal makers, and others definitely help enable the sales, but nothing happens before the salespeople initially identify the opportunities.

So far in this chapter, we have mainly addressed the needs of relationship managers, account managers, and client partners. But before the client partners get engaged, there are business development executives who open the doors in the accounts. The industry calls these salespeople by many names: hunters, sales reps, field agents. We are not interested in using one name or another; we want to discuss some of the key traits shared by all successful salespeople. Although not scientifically proven as best practices via thorough study, we believe from our experience that gaining these traits will definitely help you open doors in big accounts. But before we discuss these specific sales traits, we want to share a story about one such salesperson (see Box 3.3).

Box 3.3: The Story of One Insuppressible Mango

Until the middle of 2005, Sunil Maheshwari had it all—a nice car, a good house, a social circle of Bangalore Web 2.0 hipsters, and a promising cushy job. He was on his way to getting the corner office, running P&L (profit and loss responsibility shows bigger authority), making those "questionably important business need" types of round-the-world trips, and being the well-versed, globally traveled storyteller at the numerous naming ceremonies he went to. Then, suddenly the crazy bug stung him so hard that he temporarily lost his senses. He quit his job and confined himself to his suburban home, where he began crafting a business plan to form a company. Sunil wanted to start a company with a dream of providing the several billion forgotten people at the bottom of the pyramid (BOP) with something not on the agendas for Research in Motion, Nokia, or Motorola. He wanted to offer them the same fun cell phone experience that was reserved only for the high-end phones, but for a fraction of the price. That's how Mango was born.

Although it did not take a rocket scientist to realize that this market is a great opportunity, the venture capitalists (VCs), angel investors, and other financiers did not really see it initially. In India in early 2006, the funding of entrepreneurs was still a relatively new experience. Sunil had to literally beg for funding

(continued)

from many potential investors, but with no success. In his desperation for money to fund his venture, he asked his family and friends. He got some help, but for this kind of technology startup in Bangalore it was not sufficient for sustaining and growing the business at the same time. Like many startup owners, Sunil had three main growth problems: (1) lack of cash, (2) inability to build a core team, and (3) getting the right resources to support the core team.

These not-so-unique challenges cripple most startups, especially the ones with no VC backing. Sunil wanted to tackle the core-team challenge first, because he knew he needed the right team to build the envisioned product. He recruited the best people his money could buy, but we need to understand the challenge here. In 2006, Indian technology workers were receiving something in the region of a 25 percent annual raise from multi-national corporations (MNCs). The MNCs and the big Indian IT companies were growing at about a 40–50 percent rate, year on year. So it was easy for these companies to pay increased salaries to keep their talent. Plus, the big companies were awarding all the required perks: retirement benefits, good health insurance, and further education opportunities. And here was Mango offering high-end engineers a job that wouldn't pay well, a company that could fold in a few months, and a future that was, let's say, questionable. Sunil decided he had to be creative to fight these challenges. He offered a job to a candidate who was much needed for his company. Sunil got him on board by paying six months' salary up front. It was a bold but necessary move.

Once his small team was in place, he needed to tackle his lack of cash. He visited many Bangalore-based MNCs and desperately tried to sell them the evaluation licenses. The biggest handicap was that he had to charge for licenses when many competitors were giving them out free. The hard-nosed sales drive paid off, though. Some evaluation licenses were sold, which resulted in modest cash inflow. To keep the lights on in his company, Sunil and his team funneled the rest by doing paid consulting for other companies.

Although some basic product was there by this point, it needed more features to sell commercially. Sunil knew that for

(continued)

Mango to be successful, he had to supply the necessary resources to his team in the form of technology assets and research materials. Some of his needs were quite basic, such as needing an office space. Again an entrepreneur friend admired Sunil's drive for success and gave Mango free office space in a plug-and-play mode. Now, Mango had office space and some infrastructure support to keep doing what it intended: build mobile application and user interface frameworks for lower-end cell phones. Eventually, Mango was able to move into the Indian Institute of Management (IIM) Bangalore premises as part of IIM's incubator program. Mango now had not only a space but also access to the best minds in the business for support and guidance.

Since inception, the Mango team were tireless self-promoters working on a dime. Sunil and his business partner Lekh Joshi reached out to everybody they knew from their past lives at corporate. They constantly updated folks on their product-development status, used these networking channels to meet and greet potential customers, and campaigned through the local chapters of such organizations as the National Association of Software and Services Companies (NASSCOM) and the Indus Entrepreneurs (TiE) to get their name out into the market.

In 2008, NASSCOM recognized Mango as the leading company in innovation—quite a feat for a once-bootstrapped company formed in a bedroom. Mango now has ties with global giants such as Qualcomm, Texas Instruments, NXP, and a few tier-one, tier-two, and tier-three original equipment manufacturers. These companies are putting Mango software into their low-end, mass-market cell phones and platforms to sell them in the developing parts of the world. Sunil believes he built his *mantra* for success on three unique selling propositions (USPs): keeping costs low, keeping usability simple, and localizing solutions.

What can Sunil teach us seasoned salespeople working within the secure environment of a big company such as IBM, Accenture, or HP? Here are two lessons we believe all salespeople can learn from Sunil's story:

1. Be the creative, poor, hungry, and driven (PHD) sales force.
2. Make "common sense" not so uncommon.

Be the Creative PHD Sales Force

In our story in Box 3.3, Sunil needed an ace engineer to work for him. He knew that if he simply offered a job, the person would not come to Mango. Sunil paid six months' salary in advance as a security deposit to get this person in. It was an unconventional move to lure him to the job, and it worked.

When we talk to salespeople in our organization, we always run into brilliant individuals with "great sales potential" but average results. It's no surprise that most of these salespeople try conventional tactics to get sales. They try such methods as cold calling, e-mail campaigning, and unsolicited visits to break into new accounts. We all know how we treat the person making an unsolicited dinner-time sales phone call. The technology service delivery salespeople get the same treatment— hanging up the phone. Does creativity work in opening doors in services sales? You bet it does! (See Box 3.4.)

Unfortunately, we cannot tell you exactly how to be creative. It depends on the situation. If there were an exact formula, it would be self-defeating because everyone would use it. What worked for Sunil Maheshwari or Tony Gonzales may not work for you. But we can urge you, sincerely, to spend a lot of time analyzing your target account and brainstorming with your colleagues on how to stand out in positioning yourself while pitching. As important as it is to create a USP, we believe it is equally important to be unique in how you plan on establishing contact.

But simply being creative is not enough. Let's face it; selling into white space (a bare patch where your company has little or no presence) is possibly the most brutal selling of all. Most people do not enjoy this role, which comes with many rejections, a lot of running around, and often limited results or none. Nobody understands this better than an entrepreneur like Sunil Maheshwari. In our minds, Sunil is PHD (you'll recall: poor, hungry, and driven), or at least he behaves as though he is. He borrowed money from his family, asked for free office space from a friend, and constantly fought to work on a dime to get what he needed. During our interview with him, he also mentioned how his team did not have money to pitch these products by traveling overseas. So he and his team had the patience to wait and engage with the big companies, such as Texas Instruments or Qualcomm and others, whenever their global executives made trips to India.

Although most successful salespeople are not really poor and enjoy healthy base pay, they behave as though they are poor, hungry, and

---

Box 3.4: How Tony Tapped the Writers

Anirban has been friends with Tony Gonzales for the last eight years. He has an impeccable record of service delivery sales, bringing in deals that totaled more than US$50 million. Somehow Tony could get a whiff of an upcoming deal before most other people.

After knowing Anirban for many years, Tony finally confided how he does it. He never courts the customers directly. He also never courts the third-party advisors much. Instead, he uses a methodical relationship-building campaign with newspaper and magazine columnists who write about business in his territory. The top business writers for these publications routinely meet the CEOs, who update them about their forthcoming ventures. Tony gets to know about the high-level direction of companies from these writers long before the material is published and then uses ground-level intelligence to verify the information. His ground-level verification process is to solicit information from the project managers, programmers, and other operations people in those accounts. He shamelessly targets provider employees who are working in the account, as well as customer employees through the same channel.

It was amazing how he mastered a technique of soliciting the right information from these people and putting together a corresponding sales plan. Tony swears he has never run into another salesperson taking this approach. Tapping into business writers to get intelligence is his creation. Because Tony is a certified exaggerator we have to take his claim to fame with a pinch of salt. Nonetheless, we have to admit he was creative. How did he manage to get this information from the business writers as well as the operations people? According to Tony's own words, "It's the magic of Jim Beam [Kentucky whiskey] and Partagas [a renowned Cuban cigar]."

---

driven, with life and death depending on their effort. That may be a dramatic way of saying it, but good service delivery sales reps need to be able to create this self-inflicted pressure to perform. We are promoting an all-out sales philosophy, but let's not forget to use a bit of common sense along the way.

Make Common Sense Not So Uncommon

Creativity and gusto are great as long as they are grounded in common sense. Salespeople often grow desperate in making a sale. This hampers their ability to really think through whether their creative, gung-ho strategy is going to work at all. Anirban learned this firsthand, in a shocking way (see Box 3.5).

Box 3.5: When Stupid Creativity Backfires

Several years back, Anirban was responsible for selling software to technology companies. He used his employer's extensive research capability and internal selling network to identify that a particular consumer electronic retailer would be the perfect candidate for pitching a particular product and service Anirban was planning on selling. Further investigation also led him to the director in charge of quality assurance in this potential customer at the time. It was evident that this person would need to purchase new software and services about three financial quarters out. He was the perfect candidate to be befriended.

Anirban decided not to approach him in a conventional way. Back then, one of his favorite sales tactics with potential prospects was to send business books, once a quarter, via mail with a handwritten note that basically urged the customer to enjoy the book. Sometimes, this was followed by sending newspaper clippings of something relevant to the customer, or a business CD, or an invitation to a relevant event. About six months or so later, Anirban would call on this prospect to schedule an appointment. Even if they had thrown away everything he sent, the repeated innovative gifts would have at least bought some name recognition. This strategy worked most of the time; he would get to meet the person in his or her office.

But this time, the strategy backfired. Anirban's gift of the wrapped book was sent back to him the following day via FedEx, with a small note: "Thanks for the gift. We do not need or appreciate it. Please do not contact us." We doubt things can go much worse than this, as far as rejection is concerned.

What really happened? Anirban probably used to send about 20 packages to potential prospects at a time. Like anything else in business, as the task became more cumbersome, covering more prospects, the process itself became a commodity. Anirban outsourced the work of sending these personalized mailings to an assistant who would sign the card, pack the book, and send it out. Initially, the instructions were very specific and Anirban would spend a lot of time scouting for the book that would fit each customer's profile. In time, he got lazy; he expected the assistant to choose the right business book and send it out. His assistant did a fabulous job, until she decided to scout for famous business books that were offered at a massive discount. Nothing wrong with that strategy; it helped keep costs low. But when she found Dr. Phil's *Self Matters: Creating Your Life from the Inside Out* in the discount section for US$7 apiece, and decided to send out a number of copies, she made a blunder.

For all non-American readers: Dr. Phil is a famous TV psychologist who advises people on all sorts of matters related to emotional crises. His straight talk on self-help topics is popular among people going through such personal challenges as divorce, loss of a loved one, or bankruptcy. Although immensely popular, these books are not the kind you want to give out to a customer. They could be taken as insinuating "You are a screw-up; read this, and your life will be better." This can be especially insulting to a new person with whom you are trying to build a relationship. Anirban later heard from the client executive in the account that some people in the customer organization had actually mentioned how outraged this individual was that somebody had sent him this book.

What lessons can be learned from this story?

- *Acceptability check* Think repeatedly about whether the creative action is acceptable under business standards that prevail in your country. For example, sending a book in some countries may be looked on as a bribe.
- *Focus on the emotional quotient* Anticipate the emotional reaction of the recipient. Even if your action is acceptable, it may be offensive to certain people. These books could be popular in some places, but not others. Erring on the side of caution may be the best bet.
- *Be diligent with the little things* While being creative, never take the small tasks lightly. Anirban sowed the seeds of catastrophe by not paying attention to which books were going out.

Conclusion

What we have described so far as large-deal account-development traits or business-development methodologies that can be used to find large deals are really a *Cliff's Notes* version. The purpose of this book is to give you a taste of what is needed in the field. Once you engage deeply with the role of scouting for mega deals, you will have to lean on your own organization's best practices to go about it.

We do have a word of caution about large-deal business development. Many companies force the salespeople to meet quarterly targets. They also put salespeople on a compensation plan that rewards quarterly wins and penalizes unmet quarterly targets. It is almost impossible for salespeople to focus on large-deal business development if they are punished for their efforts and not rewarded.

Going after large deals in white space is a time-consuming strategy. In reality, it is hard for customers to switch vendors. So when a service provider goes to a potential big customer and tries to displace a well-established incumbent which has services, hardware, and software wrapped into the deal, it becomes a Herculean task. But one big win can offset the several tries that fail to produce any fruits for the labor invested.

Providers serious about getting Big Deals should invest in the long run and not focus solely on quarterly profit and loss. It takes time for Big Deals to materialize, and if salespeople are always under the gun they will never chase Big Deals. One way to get around this challenge is to create a compensation plan where large-deal business-development activities are encouraged within accounts. A portion of leveraged pay should be geared toward compensating salespeople for showing documented effort in large-deal creation. BU leaders need to allow some latitude so that large-deal business development becomes a priority.

Note

1. See http://www.datamonitor.com.

CHAPTER 4

Winning Deals Through
Third-Party Advisors

The Art of People Doing
Business with People

Selling large-scale information technology (IT) services has become more complex in the last 10 years (see Figures 4.1 and 4.2). Companies considering global sourcing are savvier and the selection of IT service providers has increased. Adding to the complexity of this sourcing mix is a breed of sourcing advisory firms called strategic sourcing consultants, or third-party advisors (TPAs), who are prominent brokers of large global sourcing deals. Although consultants or TPAs have been in existence as a sub-industry within the IT global sourcing industry since its inception, their influence on large deals has increased in the last decade. But if you analyze the scenarios closely, you will see that TPAs also help service delivery companies and providers. Service delivery companies can apply certain tactics to get into the good graces of the TPAs, and this can definitely improve their chance of finding, and winning, deals through this channel. In fact, the major IT system integrators use TPA firms as an adjunct to their business development activities.

In this chapter, we offer a few field-tested thoughts on how to win business through TPAs by using some basic people-to-people skills and Business Development 101 skills. But first, let's hear about Gary Somers (see Box 4.1).

What Gary faced in this company is not unique, in our experience. Many TPA relationship managers we talked to during the course of interviewing for this book had similar tales. The difference is that some of these people not only survived the pressure but thrived, bringing in business and building long-term relationships with the TPAs. So how did they do it? To understand how to work the TPA route, one needs to better understand the TPA business.

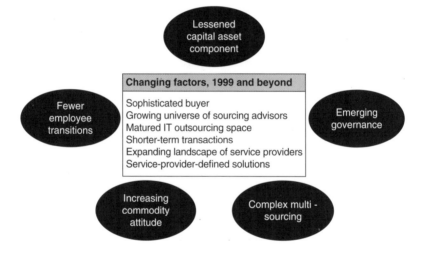

The "Old Days"
(1980s and 1990s)

Relatively autonomous buyers
Well-known sourcing advisors
Handful of major service providers
Long-term transactions
Lift and shift

Lengthy, expensive pursuits

Figure 4.1   Selling IT and Technology Services: The "Old Days"

Lessened capital asset component

Changing factors, 1999 and beyond

Sophisticated buyer
Growing universe of sourcing advisors
Matured IT outsourcing space
Shorter-term transactions
Expanding landscape of service providers
Service-provider-defined solutions

Fewer employee transitions

Emerging governance

Increasing commodity attitude

Complex multi - sourcing

Figure 4.2   Selling IT and Technology Services: Changing Factors

Box 4.1: Gary Goes Nuts!

Gary Somers had just accepted a position with a reputable, India-based, global sourcing services provider. He was American by birth, had lived in Europe and Asia, spoke three languages, and was well versed in global business. He had had a distinguished career in several sales, marketing, strategy, and IT management roles at a number of world-class IT services companies. He wrote

(continued)

and published in important magazines worldwide, spoke at top global sourcing events, and was considered a subject matter expert in the field of global sourcing. In short, he would have been a good catch for any company in this business of ours, where we are always trying to monetize through globalization.

Gary was excited about taking this role at the India-based provider. He had seen the exceptional growth of India Inc. companies, growth that was almost a rags-to-riches story. He admired India Inc.'s ability to deliver, win business, and grow at an unprecedented rate. He realized that in this grown-up phase of global sourcing, this provider would be graduating to win the big and strategic deals. This time around, Gary did not simply want a seat in the peanut gallery watching the show as a spectator; he wanted to be part of the team creating history.

Gary's view of his new role as TPA relationship manager was as a bridge between his organization and the complex world of TPAs. He wanted to positively influence the views of TPAs about his employer. He also wanted to learn from the TPAs what they were looking for in potential partners. He was keen not only on getting potential deals via these TPAs but also on bringing them into existing opportunities to play an advisory role. Gary envisioned this knowledge-driven bridge as his role, where he could be the broker of this give-and-take relationship between the TPAs and his employer. He met several senior executives from the business units, talked to corporate and support groups, and was interviewed by the CEO of the potential employer. He was glad his vision was not just shared but instead promoted by these leaders. Gary had found a great employer! Or at least that's what he thought.

The first quarter after his start was great. He went to India for the first time and experienced how the competency delivery units worked. He spent time learning about SAP and the IT support competencies of the companies and also about the people aspect of this cultural exchange as well. He returned to the U.S. excited and armed with much knowledge about his organization regarding IT delivery capability, as well as cultural knowledge (such as how big an occasion a naming ceremony in India is, compared to a first birthday party). In short, Gary was eager to share all his business and non-business lessons learned with his customers, the TPAs.

(continued)

Gary called one of the leading TPA firms to set up an appointment to talk about his company. He brought an existing name and credibility to the market, so getting an appointment was not very difficult. He walked in confidently with the global head of banking to meet this particular advisor, Bill Kirby. After shaking hands and getting his first bite at the doughnut that was offered to him, Gary wanted to start talking shop. Bill stopped him even before Gary said a word. Raising his hand, he said, "Gary, I am so glad that you came on board because now we are not going to get calls from 30 different sales reps from your organization on a monthly basis. Hope you can streamline the interactions." In the course of the meeting, Gary realized that although this TPA recognized the technical capability of his employer, they simply thought of his company as a "pain in the ass" to do business with. The BUs in his company never shared information with one another so the TPAs never got to see an integrated picture. Or every now and then, when the TPAs did get to see a holistic view, some BUs would try to bypass others by working backdoor deals with the TPA. The result was not good. The session soon degenerated into a "tell-tell" session. Bill and his other team members described how they absolutely hated that so many proposals coming from Gary's outfit had conflicting information, how data looked different, and how they were not professional. Gary was a bit offended by this point. By the time the meeting was over, he had a mental list of dos and don'ts about handling this TPA.

Four months later, the situation had worsened. But Gary did try to be an agent of change. He hurled several notifications to the sales teams on how to connect to the TPAs via him, how not to bother TPAs to the point of ticking them off, and how to write standardized proposals. The prevailing habit of "not writing standardized proposals" was a bit of a shocker to Gary. How on earth can a world-class service delivery organization send proposals that have varying look and feel, logo sizes, fonts, and most importantly information on revenue, headcount, and locations? Gary started pestering the sales teams, and they fought back. Very soon, he was receiving regular calls from the "big kahunas" of the many BUs, asking him about his value to the company and how many deals he was bringing in. Gary was also unable to stop the individual

(continued)

BUs from directly approaching the TPAs without notifying him or the others. Hence, duplication of effort and continuation of TPA dissatisfaction went on unabated. An intelligent business leader was even shocked at why Gary did not have a badge to get into the TPA offices. Her logic was, "Well, all the account managers [sales guys] have badges and open access to their clients. So, why can't a TPA relationship manager obtain the same level of access?" After working for 30 years, Gary figured he did not really need this hassle. He felt he was going nuts. One fine Friday, with no fanfare, Gary resigned.

Everything You Need to Know About TPAs

What is one of the most challenging things a salesperson can think of while selling to a non-savvy customer? Traditional wisdom may say that the challenge is when the customer brings a friend along as a guide—a friend who knows the salesperson's tricks, understands the customer's needs, and knows the product or service offering well. You may want to think of the TPA as that knowledgeable friend, advisor, or confidant. In the services business, most customers are smart, but many may not be knowledgeable about structuring core global sourcing services, for example, how to structure deals (read: pay a fair price), how to manage large programs, and how to come out with a solution that helps their customers. Have you heard the old saying that "the man who represents himself in court has a fool for a lawyer"? The same holds true for global sourcing unless your customer has highly skilled leaders on the payroll (and more firms are hiring these skills). Additionally, it is important to note that several law firms specialize in commercial global sourcing work, alongside the TPAs. Together they solve the customers' strategic and operational challenges as they relate to global sourcing. The fundamental value TPAs bring to an engagement is a *methodology* or *process* managed by highly skilled professionals, which, if followed, will result in a thorough, documented, and viable business case for global sourcing. Each TPA firm has a well-documented series of "proprietary" steps honed through years of experience, making it worth the consulting fees paid.

TPA firms cannot be overestimated for the influence they have on the ultimate sourcing decision. Many companies considering global sourcing will rely on the TPAs to "invite" capable service providers to

Figure 4.3 The Global Sourcing Players

participate in the making of a deal. TPAs can then become gatekeepers (see Figure 4.3) and exclude firms they believe have not demonstrated the requisite capabilities that their client is seeking to outsource. In some cases, the TPAs actually have a formal vote in selecting the ultimate service provider. Finally, we have seen many TPAs take a two-pronged approach in consulting customers. First, they wear a management consulting hat in prescribing actions based on pure business challenges and setting strategic direction. Second, they like to implement that recommendation by using a global sourcing strategy. Here are a few details on the *modus operandi* of TPAs:

- *Management consulting* Some TPAs work similarly to traditional management consulting firms such as McKinsey, Boston Consulting Group (BCG), and Bain by helping plan a course for strategic and operational challenges. We know of several TPAs who help customers analyze strategic objectives: entering a new market or new business; doing industry analysis; carrying out mergers and acquisitions; developing a new product, pricing strategy, or growth strategy; and creating a competitive response. We also know of TPAs that help customers with such operational challenges as increasing sales, reducing costs, improving the bottom line, and doing turnarounds. The recommendations are generally business-driven and sourcing-provider-agnostic at this point. The goal is to use these findings to prepare a work plan that includes select sourcing as a means to the end prescribed by their management consulting strategy.
- *Sourcing advisory and management* As a service provider, we have been primarily interested in the TPA's role of sourcing advice and management. This particular service is designed to implement the plan prescribed by their management consulting wing. Often, customers actually hire them just for sourcing help and not for the management consulting aspect.

All TPAs have their own methodologies on how to help choose providers and map them against the client's needs. But we have seen that they all follow variations of the same basic flow:

Sourcing analysis→Sourcing implementation→Sourcing management

Sourcing Analysis

Typically, TPAs take the business case (done by management consultants or done in-house) and develop a strategy to align technology with business drivers. The existing business architecture is studied on a high level and a future-state architecture diagram is created. The diagrams are generally business-design-focused and not technical-architecture-focused. Finally, this is where it is decided how TPAs will select vendors. TPAs work with their clients to make a decision using requests for proposal (RFPs), requests for information (RFIs), or other business-case-driven processes to solicit service providers for the work to be performed.

Sourcing Implementation

In this phase, TPAs work closely with customers to analyze their lower-level sourcing needs. Assessment and analysis regarding IT value, IT portfolio, infrastructure, services, processes, and financial health are well understood. Much focus is given to transition approaches and future state. The actual RFP or business case seeking help is written and sent out to potential providers.

Sourcing Management

Here, TPAs receive the proposals back from vendors. They arrange proposal defense workshops, which include presentations, to ensure the right fit. A contract is developed and negotiated with the vendors. The goal is to help the customer engage with one or more providers as their sourcing partners. A few TPAs also want to stay engaged with the customer to become the governance authorities or program managers, thereby gaining residual income from the account.

Some of these TPAs handle the entire gamut of business activities, some focus mainly on the management consulting side, and some focus purely on sourcing advice. Some research and analysis firms, such as

Gartner and Forrester, also have a process for global sourcing and are therefore also categorized as TPAs. The industry calls TPAs by fancy names (full service outsourcing and offshoring advisors, boutique global sourcing advisory firms), or simply management consultants.

It is almost impossible to find a standard ranking of advisors or TPAs. Many organizations furnish a ranking based on their own criteria. Some of the TPAs we have worked with in the past are Technology Partners (acquired in 2008 by Information Services Group, ISG), Everest Group, NeoIT, EquaTerra (now owns Morgan Chambers), Ovum, Pace Harmon, Alsbridge, Forrester, Gartner, Nathanson and Company, and the W Group. Law firms associated with TPAs include Mayer Brown, Jones Day, Pillsbury (Shaw Pittman), and Bird and Bird (to mention just a few, because it is not unusual for many more law firms to be employed as outside counsel on these deals, even if there is no TPA involved).

Now for the surprise: *TPAs are people too!* Typically, TPAs hire consultants and researchers from top business schools. Many of the financial business-case experts are young MBA graduates who enjoy a good conversation at the coffee machine or water cooler. They also hire known industry leaders such as former COOs and CIOs who know a domain, technology, or business. Many of these consultants have more than 10 years' industry experience in service delivery, transition, transformation, business-process modeling, and program management. These consultants also bring the relationship savvy that is needed to align the customer with the provider at multiple levels. Just like you, they also have families, spouses, and significant others that can too often get lost in this rat race of fast, big money and global travel.

An interesting note is that you will find many TPA firms have a global network of offices and associates. They are practicing what they preach and offering big prizes in new engagements. Finally, many TPAs use the consulting-based partner "double-duty accountability" model whereby they are working an engagement but must also look out for their next client. Some TPA firms get hard-knuckle sales reps to knock on doors to get business. The TPAs will scout the market for potential leads that are ripe for outsourcing services. These are typically Fortune 1000 companies, but now they are also looking aggressively into the mid-market spaces. Companies with recent top executive management changes, companies that are losing money quarter after quarter, companies that have a large base of high-cost employees, and companies with low earnings before interest, taxes, depreciation, and amortization (EBITDA) are perfect candidates for TPAs to probe. TPAs use cold calls, and they partner with private equity firms to use their research wing to find these potential targets.

Today, the services delivery industry is seeing a plethora of independent TPAs who are often a one-man shop. Typically, these companies are formed by former CIOs and CTOs who have been through the global sourcing wringer. These former corporate executives mainly find customers among their associate circles. Don't get us wrong: they may be small, but they tend to pick up important accounts. The bottom line is that all of the TPAs mentioned in this chapter have been very professional, fair, and open in their dealings with the service providers working with their clients.

How Can I Win Business Through TPAs?

TPA relationship management from an emerging service provider's point of view is in its infancy, while seasoned global systems integrators have fine-tuned these relationships over many years. Relationships need to be managed at all levels, from the CEO of a 10-partner firm to the deal partners physically working on and negotiating deals. The key here is the art of people doing business with people. As with any valuable asset, you need to invest your time and energy in getting to know these people (see Box 4.2).

Box 4.2: Two Tales of Why TPA Relationships Work

Hetzel has worked on both sides of global sourcing as the project co-leader of the Hughes-Raytheon mega-outsourcing deal in 1999, a few years before the now popular "global sourcing" initiatives. First, he was on the buy side, working for Raytheon to secure the deal, and subsequently being tasked with managing it during its first year, a tremendous learning experience at all stages. After a brief career detour, he moved into the sell side of the business working for CSC, as the lead negotiator on several large- and mega-sized deals.

He has learned a lot from his TPA counterparts. First, his best personal and professional relationship was with an unnamed TPA executive with whom he interacted for nearly two years

(continued)

---

before seeing the first invitation to bid. Many sales managers might think that those two years were a waste of time. They were, if you value only short-term benefits. But after those two years, Hetzel was invited to bid for every deal where his company had the capability as a provider. He didn't win them all, but the gate was open so long as his company was willing to play ball and receive regular feedback on the good and bad of their engagements (just as we would give feedback to others).

Having learned this investment lesson early in his career at GM, Hetzel "invests" his time and energy in those partners, associates, and executive assistants (who run most of the TPA firms) so that he can get to know them as people. He checks on the status of their significant others (occasionally including them in business functions as well) and reschedules appointments to accommodate their personal needs. It sounds a lot like a "sales" job, but remember these TPAs represent some of your future customers.

The second story involves a TPA that remained involved in a client engagement years after the initial deal was negotiated. This was because the two parties were constantly bickering over contract interpretations. Hetzel, and some of his teammates, were kept around to "facilitate" the transition and transformation activities. He would regularly get short emails explaining a "flare-up" at the client site, in which the TPA would ask him to give his unofficial views on the issues. Because Hetzel was the lead negotiator for the deal on the service provider side, the TPA expected some insight from Hetzel. These exchanges were sanity checks for the TPA, though Hetzel's sought-after unofficial remarks were no different from what he would have given as an official reading. Well, during those exchanges of emails that lasted nearly two years, Hetzel never got an invitation to any of this TPA's deals (because the TPA didn't have any new ones)! However, many of the other advisors from the same TPA firm called Hetzel to invite his company to their deals instead.

To be clear, these personal, yet professional, relationships were always above reproach, with no extraordinary gifting, special treatment, bending of engagement rules to share information, ever. Even so, professional and personal respect investments go a long way to enhancing your career, and many times even personal associations.

Since we first started working with TPAs back in the day, we have seen many changes in this space. They have a lot to do with an industry that is ever evolving. So we decided to get an expert's opinion on the best way to connect with this breed—the ones that can make providers flourish by bringing Big Deals.

We wanted to find a subject matter expert to talk about this topic of TPA relationship management, someone who had worked on projects from the services-provider side as well as the TPA side. We wanted this person to be an authority on global sourcing, and most importantly, a student of this space. We found that superhuman in Tom Tunstall, who is currently the TPA relationship advisor for a major IT service provider. His responsibilities are exactly the same as those of Gary, who was featured in an earlier story (see Box 4.1). In the past, he worked as business development manager for Everest Group, where he was responsible for bringing in TPA business. Tom is also the co-chair of the Dallas Chapter of the International Association of Outsourcing Professionals (IAOP) and the author of *Outsourcing and Management: Why the Market Benchmark Will Topple Old School Management Styles*. Tom brings a lot of buy-and-sell-side global sourcing experience, having worked in this space in the U.S. and also in Afghanistan, Argentina, Brazil, El Salvador, Kenya, Mexico, and Zambia. He wrote his Ph.D. dissertation on global sourcing.

Rules for Success in Getting Deals Through TPAs

Tom gave us four pointers that he thinks can help a relationship manager in managing TPAs. We put them in the context of our collective experience of working with TPAs as part of large organizations.

Rule one: Set internal expectations
Rule two: Practice *quid pro quo*
Rule three: Be the guide
Rule four: Be visible

Rule One: Set Internal Expectations—But Do It Diplomatically!

It is impossible to keep all business stakeholders happy in this TPA relationship manager role. Let's analyze why. Typically, large service-delivery companies capable of doing Big Deals have about 10 market-facing verticals and 10 competency-based horizontals. Now, almost all companies have some strong verticals and horizontals and some not-so-strong ones. The TPA relationship manager obviously promotes the stronger ones to get the deals. Often, the weaker verticals and horizontals try to feed off the stronger ones. But what is the problem in this approach? The BU leaders heading these weaker verticals or horizontals want to win more deals, and the TPA relationship manager constantly pushes back. So you usually have a raft of business leaders who feel that having a TPA relationship manager is a waste of time. In addition to this, there are many business leaders who believe that the role of TPA relationship manager is really no more than a mixture of telesales and field sales. We believe that a good TPA relationship manager needs to be adept at managing these internal expectations before managing external demands. Here are some actions that good TPA relationship managers take to manage internal expectations.

- *Push them back* Good TPA relationship managers are masters at pushing back with the BUs on what is reasonable and what is not, as far as deal-seeking expectations are concerned. For example, if a weak BU of a large service provider wants to get in on a deal, sometimes it is important for the TPA relationship manager to dissuade the BU leader from pursuing it. Why? Too many losses bring bad credibility, resulting in negative perception. In the TPA business, perception is king.
- *Practice self-promotion* Good TPA relationship managers are masters at promoting what they do. They send out success stories, status updates and the like to the right people in the organization, letting them know about how their channel is adding value to the bottom line. This self-promotion is not just important, but also essential. It is hard to measure TPA relationship manager success. A good TPA leader can bring in many RFIs and RFPs, but the win rate for those invitations can be low. Is the loss because the teams were incompetent and the solution requested was not matched by the solution given? Or did the losses happen because the TPA relationship manager simply called on a TPA advisor friend to secure an invitation to bid, and the RFI or RFP was given as a favor from that friend, who had no intention of actually awarding it to the company? How do you establish what the real reason was? How can you convincingly prove that the TPA relationship manager is doing his or her job? Our research shows that there is always this ambiguity. It is

up to the TPA relationship manager to define the success criteria and promote achievements to the greatest extent possible.

- *Manage TPA contact mechanism* Most important, good TPA relationship managers succeed in influencing BUs not to bother the TPAs. They are able to establish a systematic method of TPA contact and relationship nurturing. All BUs then go through this centralized process for contacting TPAs. It is funny how it is generally accepted by all that only a company's corporate relations people contact and maintain relationships with Wall Street analysts. So why do the all the BUs have a propensity to call TPAs directly and not use the single source of a TPA relationship manager? Why treat the TPA relationship any different from the analyst relationship?

Rule Two: *Quid Pro Quo*—It's a Life of Give-and-Take, Baby

In simple terms, give-and-take is a fact of life. You do something for me, and I will return the favor. Although TPAs are supposed to be neutral (and they are), they are also still human. Their core human tendency of practicing *quid pro quo* is more obvious when the economy is down and the deal opportunities are rare. Note: TPAs expect you to bring them into business as much as you expect them to bring you in. So what can a TPA relationship manager do to facilitate *quid pro quo* with TPAs?

- *Engage known TPAs in established accounts* It is obvious why a sales leader in an established account would be hesitant to bring in a TPA to "evaluate" his or her work. Essentially, TPAs assess service providers. But not all TPAs are the same as far as service providers are concerned. All service providers have a good relationship with some of the TPAs known to them. There is mutual trust and understanding in these cases. Why not bring in some of your ally TPAs to help your trusted customers? These customers are the ones with whom you have good business (preferably annuity-based as opposed to project-based business). Why not let these TPAs install some governance within the customer base so that everyone can benefit? TPA relationship managers should work hard to convince BU leaders about the benefits of bringing in trusted TPAs in established accounts.
- *Inform high-value TPAs about "low-propensity-to-win" deals* A thorough bid-no-bid analysis should establish which deals are not

a good bet for your company. Although the temptation may be to bid on everything that moves, encourage your BUs to differentiate between deals with high or low propensity to win. Why not tell the high-value TPAs, the ones bringing in a lot of deals, about these low-propensity opportunities, especially in low-penetration accounts? Even if another TPA is working the deal, you can still inform your preferred TPA about it so they have a shot at the deal as well. What do you have to lose if this TPA comes in and takes over the account?

* *Seek a TPA as a referee* Let's face it, there are some accounts that may be large and strategic but that you wish did not exist. These customers nitpick about everything you do, constantly micro-manage, and believe they know it all. Sometimes it takes forever to close a deal with them, simply because the sales evaluation is so cumbersome. These are also ideal situations in which to engage TPAs who can streamline the buy process. Sometimes the TPAs can actually sell their credibility better here, with their Ivy League grads on staff and their walking-billboard-style promotions. Even if you lose deals initially, a shorter sales cycle will at least help you in accurately forecasting revenues for each quarter.

Rule Three: Be the Guide—and Form a Bridge

It's no coincidence that a lot of TPA relationship managers working for big service delivery organizations are former deal makers or BU heads. This is also a coaching role. Many good TPA relationship managers do webinars, seminars, and other sessions fairly regularly to coach business teams on how to write proposals and respond to RFPs in a way that is TPA-friendly.

The sales and deals experience of these TPA relationship managers brings credibility. Deal teams are more likely to listen to a person they perceive as having "been there and done that," as opposed to somebody who is preaching on the basis of theoretical knowledge.

Many of these experienced hands take things further. They are also efficient in coaching the TPAs on how to interact with their employers. They assume the role of trusted advisor to the TPAs, as well as giving them a true picture of their own organization. If this sounds like playing for both sides, it is, to some extent. These individuals truly integrate the TPA-vendor chemistry by becoming the bridge between the service organization and the TPA.

Rule Four: Be Visible—by Being in the Right Place and Doing the Right Things

If we survey the IAOP chapters, NASSCOM divisions, and Project Management Institute (PMI) chapters, we see a lot of visible individuals. These visible people are the ones presenting, and speaking, at national or chapter events. They are also publishing in industry journals and newsletters. They are perceived to be knowledgeable. If you investigate closely, you will find that many of them are in some alliance-building role, such as TPA relationship management, product-alliance management, or industry-alliance management. Why is that? The right visibility in these forums brings instant credibility. It is this credibility or SME status that makes the partners want to engage with these people. Although this is not a must-have skill, we believe that this attribute will help TPA relationship managers penetrate further into their TPA targets.

Conclusion

The best way to summarize what works with regard to capitalizing on a TPA lead channel is described by the anecdote in Box 4.3.

Box 4.3: How Subu Paved the Way for Neelam

Subu is a promising software engineer working for a major telecom service provider in Dallas. He comes from a conservative Brahmin (Indian caste) family from Chennai. While pursuing his M.S. in engineering in a local U.S. university, Subu met the beautiful Neelam, who grew up in Mumbai and had a liberal upbringing. Although Subu and Neelam were as different as two people can be, they complemented each other with their unique values and outlooks on life.

When Subu told his parents that he was going to marry Neelam, they agreed. However, they had a completely different idea about what sort of wife Neelam should be. Right after the marriage, they expected him to force her to do certain things that many people might find unreasonable. Two such drastic requests were for her to quit wearing Western clothes forever and to limit

(continued)

---

interaction with other men. Although it may be a reasonable expectation in some situations, the expectations were almost impossible for Neelam to fulfill, even if she were a willing candidate. She works for a TV station, where she has both male and female colleagues and also some guidelines on corporate clothing while on duty.

Subu, being the engineer that he was, negotiated a methodical "Neelam can do list" with his parents. He was able to also convince her to start doing some of these things, even though she was not thrilled about it. In return for this favor, Subu also did a lot of extra nice things for Neelam that she never expected him to do. He was also relentless in promoting to his parents what Neelam did for him and vice versa. He was present at as many family events as possible, for both his side of the family and hers. Last but not least, he constantly guided Neelam and his parents to avoid stepping on those unintentional family landmines (every married person knows what we are saying) to reduce friction.

Although Subu's parents and Neelam may not agree on many things, they have learned to work out a successful understanding. At the time of writing this book, they have been married for eight years and have three children.

Here are the lessons learned from the story in Box 4.3:

- *Set internal expectations* Subu was able to set the right expectations with his "Neelam can do list" for the internal stakeholders (the parents) with regard to what Neelam (the TPA) can or cannot do.
- *Quid pro quo* He also did a lot of nice and unexpected work for Neelam in return for some special favors. It was a give-and-take relationship.
- *Be the guide* Subu helped both his parents and Neelam avoid family landmines to reduce friction.
- *Be visible* He used every opportunity to mingle at family events, to be a person that both sides liked and trusted.

In summary, it should be abundantly clear from both the client sell side and service provider buy side that in the services business it is all about people, for they are the true competitive differentiators.

DOING DEALS

CHAPTER 5

Leading from the Rear

Influence Events and Lead the Deal

"Leading from the rear" has only one objective: leading without glory or explicit control. We have all seen good leaders being able to influence others while not having any official stamp of control. Why did millions of people join Gandhi's non-violence movement or support Nelson Mandela's fight against apartheid? Gandhi and Mandela were masters at influencing people. In business, there are many Gandhis and Mandelas who influence the people around them every day to achieve desirable results. However, unlike Gandhi and Mandela, these leaders do not become heroes. They influence others to achieve victories by staying out of the limelight.

Understanding your role in the company hierarchy is critical to accomplishing overall business objectives. Are you the person who needs direct control over new business pursuits, with the dedicated assets and decision authority required to complete the tasks? Or are you OK with indirect control (you have the charter for increasing new business), where the decisions and some significant assets are owned by others? Pursuing and closing large deals requires the involvement of many people across several departments of an organization, among them finance, legal, and operations, as well as multiple industry vertical business units. Regardless of your company structure, there will be a need for leaders with strong collaboration skills to lead the deal teams from the rear. Strong Type A personalities, such as superstar salespeople or many "C" level executives and technical leaders, require explicit control to lead their teams and demand overt recognition of their success. In fact, many compensation formulas reward this behavior through significant variable compensation structures. However, working in multi-disciplined, cross-functional, and non-dedicated teams brings about the need for special collaboration skills; leading from the rear is about the personal skills and confidence to lead the team to greatness, without personal fanfare or notoriety. This chapter focuses on the core ingredients that deal team members must possess in order to succeed at guiding the rest of the organization to win mega deals.

Angie Morgan and Courtney Lynch describe the leadership qualities of successful women leaders in their book *Leading from the Front: No-Excuse Leadership Tactics for Women.*[1] A trait that they do not cover is one that we call leading from the rear. It was once popular in politics to suggest that behind every successful man was a woman pulling the strings—Martha Washington, Eleanor Roosevelt, Coretta Scott King, and Nancy Reagan, to mention a few. Even recent American politics, without a gender reference in the George W. Bush era, can relate to this. How many times have you heard through the media that a lot of Bush's key signature decisions were not really his, but decisions made by exceptionally brilliant politicians who chose to stay in the background? Politicians such as Dick Cheney and Karl Rove were masters at leading from the rear.

In business, a similar scenario is prevalent in successful organizations. When Satyam's former chairman interviewed Hetzel to lead the foray into closing large deals, he asked one question that Hetzel internalized as his key to success for both parties in this new global venture: "Are you comfortable joining hands with our P&L businesses where they will clearly receive the visible benefits and recognition for your collective accomplishments?" The message was clear; the success of the Strategic Deals Group would be measured by the success of others. To win a large deal, the core, large-deals bid-team members should be exceptional in making things happen from the background, without hogging the limelight. Leading from the rear is a learned skill that is not only important but also mandatory for deal makers to possess if they are to win large deals. It is also critical to note that a successful individual salesperson does not necessarily make a good sales leader. As we pointed out in the opening chapter of the book, closing large deals is a *team* sport. For American football fans: we were reminded of the word *team* in "team sports" recently. Mike Singletary, a superstar linebacker with the Chicago Bears in the 1980s and a member of the Pro Football Hall of Fame, was recently promoted to be the head coach of the San Francisco 49ers. This new role as "large deal" leader of the big team was not lost on Mike, who, even as an individual superstar in the 1980s, knew that it was the team who ultimately won the Super Bowl. In his first game as head coach, he benched and ultimately dismissed from the game altogether another superstar who refused to give up his own glory in support of the team. He believed that superstars who cannot give up individual glory in favor of the team have no place on this team. His words resonate and could be the mantra of this chapter. We have no room to work with individual superstars who want to constantly hog the limelight. The head coach of that winning Chicago Bears team in the 1980s was Mike Ditka, who required three attributes of those he wanted on his team (he called them "ACEs"):

- *Attitude* They are ready to win, ready to work, ready to do what is needed to get the job done.
- *Character* They are confident, solid, supportive individuals who do not need ego inflation.
- *Excellence* They strive to be the best they can be and work for the ultimate success of the team.

Successful deal teams are filled with ACEs.

Box 5.1: Chuck's Lesson: Sales Excellence Is Not Deals Excellence

Chuck was a fantastic salesman of software tools. He attained his sales quota every year for five years in a row. He had been successfully using his southern charm—the lone-ranger, gun-slinging style of doing business, coupled with a sweet Texas drawl—to win the hearts and minds of his customers. He was extremely proud of his knack for opening doors in uncharted territories, finishing quick sales, and moving on to the next target account—or "conquest," as he fondly though respectfully called them. After being sales rep of the year for five years in a row in the southwestern U.S. region, and consistently getting innovative awards (such as "rep on fire") from his management, Chuck figured it was time to up the ante and move into the world of large-deal outsourcing sales. He urged his organization to transfer him into the service delivery outsourcing division. On day one of his new job as large deals director, he walked into the office with the utmost confidence. After all, he was an expert salesman.

Nine months later, the situation was quite different. Chuck sat embarrassed in front of Ron, the senior vice president of his large deals group. Ron was shocked how Chuck was unable to get the support needed from participating organizations, such as IT service

(continued)

delivery, consulting, and testing services, to promote their company as unified in front of the customer and get a winning bid in.

Chuck was sitting there contemplating one question: Why on earth would a sales star be responsible for lobbying internally, playing politics, and aligning the different objectives of competing organizations to write a proposal? He had always been successful in responding to proposals alone, defending them in customer meetings with great theatrics, and finally closing the deal with much flair. He was puzzled, however, at how this approach of running solo had not yielded any results yet.

Sound familiar? Do you know a Chuck? Most of us seasoned veterans of services sales organizations have seen plenty of Chucks. These guys are great door openers or hunters, fantastic at making new sales. They are also great at closing deals that are generally project-based, reporting to a single, customer-authorized leader who can approve deals within that customer organization, oftentimes with a single signature. The dynamics of pursuing large deals are significantly different; the whole process has much more visibility and requires multiple approvals to award the deal. These deals are also multi-faceted, needing input from many organizations, followed by subsequent evaluations. What many organizations do, mistakenly, is promote individual superstars without truly going over the job requirements for roles where they need to lead as well as sell, as in a large deals team. It should be specifically noted as well that an individual superstar does not necessarily make a good leader.

The Anatomy of Leading from the Rear

Leading from the rear focuses on a few essential business leadership traits:

1. *Collaboration and unification* The ability to connect opposing forces
2. *Representative entrepreneurship* Making independent decisions that are game changers for others
3. *Consulting advisor* Bringing out the coach in someone
4. *Managing chaos* The ability to constantly guess what is coming up around the curve

Collaboration and Unification: The Ability to Connect Opposing Forces

In most system integrators and IT service providers, there are many stakeholders in each new-business pursuit. Examples of these businesses are units commonly called industry verticals, such as telecoms, banking, health care, and oil and gas. Similarly, these organizations also have service line-focused businesses called horizontals. Examples of horizontal units are SAP practice, the Application Development and Support Group, testing services, and infrastructure management services. Then there are region-centric groups that focus on certain geographies such as Europe, Asia-Pacific, and Latin America, geographies that force companies to bring in local language proficiency. Finally, there are support units (such as the Strategic Deals Group, finance, and legal) who help craft the deal. When large deals surface, these organizations have to work together to make things happen. Sound complicated? Think of an orchestra and you'll get the picture; many individual experts can play grand music only under the direction of a skilled conductor (see Box 5.2).

Box 5.2: Deal Making Begins at Home: Influencing the Internal Organization First

A major travel and logistics firm released an RFP, with the assistance of a third-party advisor, to seek proposals for managing its IT applications. As part of the deal, a major enterprise resource planning (ERP) package implementation was required.

Once invited to bid, a deal team was immediately organized with team members from all the representative units (SAP practice, the Application Development and Support Group, testing services, and infrastructure management services). The deal team was officially led by the region and vertical business representatives. An SDG leader was also added to the team to provide expert guidance.

Now with nearly 20 members, the deal team began the task of preparing a proposal to meet the customer's objectives better than the competition could (in this case, it included IBM, Infosys, and TCS in the final rounds of negotiations). Because the SDG leader was present for the first time during this process, the other

(continued)

members largely ignored his initial input and suggestions. Also, with declared positional authority residing with the vertical business unit, the SDG team member could offer only "suggestions and comments". What ensued over the course of the six-month engagement was a typical success, but achieved only through leading from the rear.

After the initial proposal, submission bidders were invited in to walk through detailed presentations of their offer. The pursuit team painstakingly prepared and rehearsed the material. At key points during the preparation, the SDG leader offered suggestions to the team that were based on his previous experience of working with the TPA that was assisting this potential customer. Most suggestions were ignored (such as preparing a special creative financial briefing; instead they extolled technical virtues).

After these briefings, the TPA and the client offered feedback for improving the next exchanges. Only after this feedback did the SDG leader win a true seat at the deal team table. Amazingly, the TPA suggestions echoed the SDG leader's unheeded advice. Make no mistake, pursuit teams hate to lose—so they quickly embraced this newfound leader from the SDG and followed his subtle leads. The financials were improved, the contract terms were refreshed, and the always-sound technical merits kept Satyam in the game to the very final rounds.

Only one factor seemed to be keeping the team from a clear, decisive win. The SDG leader had suggested that an industry expert be hired to round out the final account team that would be responsible for this client, but the vertical lead was reluctant to make the commitment (what if we hire someone and still lose the bid?). The ultimate power in leading from the rear is available only through executive reinforcement. Because so much had been invested by the organization at this stage, and timing was urgent, a call was made by the SDG leader to the chairman, who had regular contact with the team. The call was to explain the need for a key industry expert to be added to the team. Without hesitation, he authorized the hire. Satyam won the deal and began the process of learning from the leader in the rear.

How did the large deals leader, faced with the contrasting goals of several BUs and the difficult, sometimes irritable, personalities of these Type A business leaders, succeed in coordinating a unified response? Unfortunately, there are no easy steps to success here. But there are some rules that we believe should be followed to align opposing forces.

Rule One: Handle with Care

Most organizations are fragile while powerful BUs are fighting one another. We have never seen an organization (on the buy side or the sell side) that did not have internal politics. As the owners of large deal pursuits, we have to figure out a way to work through it.

We have often seen professionals, from the two opposite ends of the spectrum, at odds with each other while trying to navigate the organization. At one end, you have the bulldozers. These people typically take the "might is right" approach, pulling rank, playing politics, and confronting directly to push their own agenda without thinking of the political volatility of the situation. At the other end of the spectrum, we see leaders who are "pleasers." These are the Ms. or Mr. Congenialities of the world, who take a service-minded approach to dealing with things. They avoid confrontation, agree with all sides, and live by the *mantra* of using inaction to resolve issues.

Although the latter approach to dealing with organizational dynamics is to our minds better than the former, we recommend a path down the middle. It is best to keep all sides happy by finding the middle ground if possible. However, it is impossible to do so on every occasion. On important deal-killer items (decisions that can make or break a deal), push your agenda through, but not directly. Good leaders, in this case, use allies in the organization—internal and external channels as well as power brokers—to get their agenda across. Sometimes, you need to confront important leaders directly. When you do, focus on the issue and not on the person. Married people can relate to this last point. Have you ever disliked a decision your spouse made? You confront directly and, instead of talking about the issue and why you dislike it, you end up dealing with the issue as though it were a character flaw on your partner's part. The fight soon grows personal and ends up with one of you sleeping on the couch at night. Business fights can develop the same way, but in such cases the couch is the "non-billable bench," which has to be avoided at all costs.

Rule Two: The Ability to Engage the Right Binding Agent

Our experiences have taught us to bring in the right "binding agent" when we encounter too many opposing forces blocking a common mission. The binding agent can be a superior power, such as a CEO or managing director. In Box 5.2, the team could not always resolve issues quickly. It was imperative to get the chairman involved to make a go-no-go call for everybody. The warring parties may not agree, but they have to listen to a superior. The intervention was required and properly exercised for the good of the mission.

Rule Three: Creating Group Security

Why do educated, highly intelligent people not do what is obviously beneficial for the company? Our collective experience in working for Satyam, IBM, Sprint, GM, CSC, and other organizations has taught us that most group resistance comes from insecurity. It is the fear of being sidelined or marginalized that stops most groups from collaborating or working together. One must-have quality that large deal leaders should bring to the table is the ability to create group security. Deal makers need to make groups feel special; constantly making them feel wanted is an art that can help mend broken fences. This praise should be in the form of sincere acknowledgment of team camaraderie and spirit. False attempts or back-door manipulations will not succeed.

Rule Four: Anti-celebrity

We encourage you to actively shy away from stardom in glory, and vice versa. Consider a CEO's story (see Box 5.3).

Box 5.3: The Quiet CEO: Scott's Tale

One of the greatest leaders Anirban knows is Scott Sheffield, the CEO of Pioneer Resources, a leading oil services company. Anirban knew Scott for a good two years, playing tennis with him once a week, before he realized what role Scott had at Pioneer. Some members of the elite club in Dallas were happy tooting their own horn (and justifiably so, in a membership base that had so many

(continued)

CEOs). Scott, on the other hand, is a master at keeping an extremely low profile. In the course of 10 years of knowing him, Anirban has heard many leadership stories involving Scott and how he managed the big endeavors that his company pursued. What was most remarkable about all those stories was how he was able to distance himself from taking the leading role in any of these achievements. He has always created an environment where the focus (read: the hero worship) is not on him but on other team members. When things go south, however, Scott has the courage to take center stage and accept the blame, while assuring stakeholders with well-defined corrective action. The end result: Scott has created an army of loyalists who can feel secure and comfortable working for the greater good of the company.

What Scott teaches us is that to truly lead a complex group, one must be comfortable in one's own shoes. It is extremely important to be able to lead a dynamic group by staying out of the limelight and avoid hogging credit. However, one also needs to be brave enough to step forward, take blame if justified, and shelter the group if things do not go as planned.

If deal makers want to be revered, they are in the wrong profession. We have seen many top-notch IT executives completely sidelined in no time once they started competing head-on with BU leaders to get the glory.

Representative Entrepreneurship: Game-Changing Decision Making

Entrepreneurship within a workforce sounds great! But the real definition of entrepreneurship within a workforce is what we call "representative entrepreneurship." Under this concept, you are an entrepreneur making game-changing decisions on behalf of other people. Let us illustrate this with an example.

Imagine leading a deal team during negotiation. You are negotiating on a common matter: penalties for missed service level agreements (SLAs). This item includes agreements on time, cost, work product guarantees, or other commitments that your organization promises a customer. Typically, if SLAs are not met, the customer escalates the issue and charges a penalty.

Now let's assess your position as a member of a deal team. You are negotiating on behalf of several BUs with varying tolerance for paying penalties. A deal team cannot arbitrarily promise penalties to the customer because delivery units have to buy into the commitment. Oftentimes, during closed-door negotiations, you have to agree to give more penalties if you are to get something else. Your move may be highly justified for the greater good of the company, but it negatively affects one or more of the BUs within the company. You do not have the luxury of going back to the individual delivery units and getting buy-in one by one. In an ideal world, this is not a problem. In reality, you may have to endure painful, threatening, and sometimes career-hampering moves on the part of the BU leaders who may have been negatively affected by your decision. As a representative entrepreneur, you have to deal with these decision dilemmas and consequences frequently. You do need to ensure one thing, though: the legal expert representing you should make certain that your decision is not taking on any added legal risk above and beyond the accepted risk tolerance level of your organization.

Here are some rules of engagement we like to follow in operating successfully as representative entrepreneurs:

- *Ethics and legality check* First we assess whether what we are proposing or agreeing to is ethical and legal. We do not move forward under any circumstances if we find the action unethical or illegal.
- *The greater good of the company* If the proposed action is legal and ethical, we then like to find out whether our organization will be better off as a whole by enforcing that action.
- *Instincts* We should value our instincts. Experience has taught us that we can quantifiably map all our positions, rate them from high to low-priority, and agree or disagree on the basis of a pre-meditated plan of action; but instincts play a vital role when we are making game-changing decisions. Instincts, however, get better with experience.
- *Cojones* The actual meaning for the Spanish word *cojones* is border-line vulgar. But the real meaning of it is having the guts to do the right thing, which may be uncommon or seemingly unwise. We do not know, other than in terms of guts, how to describe Roger Federer hitting a backhand pass against Rafael Nadal while down a match point late in the fifth set after playing for more than four hours during the 2008 Wimbledon Men's Singles finals. Guess what? As deal makers, you will be expected to have the guts to make that passing shot time and time again in your daily decision making.

Consulting Advisor: Bringing out the Coach in Someone

Apart from being able to do the job successfully, deal team members need to display two major characteristics:

- *Cultural adaptation* Fitting with the existing corporate and BU culture
- *Articulation* Deal team members have to constantly articulate strategy and operation plans to a varied set of people. Many members of the audience do not have the same understanding about deal making as the team members. There are also some in the audience who are master deal makers, technology analysts, and so on. So the deal team members are expected to present the message in different formats to different categories of people. They need to have the patience and ability to help a broad, diverse group understand the intended message, and in many cases get their buy-in.

Box 5.4: Mary's Dilemma: Coach or Consultant?

We know of an exceptionally bright financial strategist. We will call her Mary for the purposes of this anecdote. Basically, financial strategists build financial models that help define the structure of the deal. These models are really a mixture of science and art. The science part is creation of the algorithm; the art part is putting it in the context of the business. Mary was great at both the science and the art of the job. She understood the business, knew how to maneuver numbers, made justifiable assumptions, and correctly created the right base case to optimize price. However, as good as she was, there were many times when business units interfacing with the deal team did not really trust her judgment, doubted her capabilities and intentions, and were reluctant to engage her on a broader scale. How is this scenario possible? What could Mary have done to change this perception of her?

Cultural Adaptation

It may sound obvious that one needs to adapt to the corporate culture when working in an organization. In this complex world of team dynamics, a common problem for deal teams is that they interface with multiple BUs who display many mini-corporate cultural traits. This phenomenon is much more common these days, with knowledge workers spreading around the globe and working from home, hotel room, and airport lounge.

Groups or teams within a company meet face-to-face periodically to form their own culture. These groups often do not identify with the core corporate culture (or at least what the culture was intended to be). Sometimes, these individual group cultures are diametrically opposed to the core company culture.

We have seen that it is much easier if deal team members adapt to the existing BU culture when they are engaging with it. Any instance of working contrary to the prevailing culture can have detrimental consequences of non-alignment, mistrust, and non-integration. This dance is harder if many of the groups that are present display diverse dynamics and culture. One needs to be an exceptional student of observation to spot the dominant group dynamic within the myriad other dynamics and align with it subtly. However, if the business behavior within a culture exhibited by a particular group is self-defeating, a deal team member must try everything in his or her power to subtly influence change for the greater good of the company, without burning bridges. It is also important to learn to choose these battles. Anybody with a teenager at home can attest to this. You can't criticize all bad behavior but probably have to pick, choose, and prioritize the ones to go for. For example, at our previous employer, Satyam, many BUs want to bid on everything that comes their way. There had not been widespread use of thorough bid-no-bid analysis. Consistently bidding on low-propensity-to-win deals only increases the cost of sales and the number of losses. We believe that the SDG at Satyam has been able to change this prevailing business behavior of bidding on everything in many BUs.

Articulation

Deal team members have the unenviable task of satisfying many stakeholders: multiple corporate bosses, the heads of BUs, delivery leaders, practice executives, and other deal-team members. Many of these people come from diverse backgrounds and have varied skill sets. They may need to have the intricacies of deal decisions explained to them because these decisions will affect them immensely. Sometimes, deal team members need to share and explain what they are doing to a lay audience and consequently have to "dumb it down."

In Box 5.4, we see that although Mary was highly skilled at her job, she also had little of something Americans colloquially term "b.s. tolerance." When she saw consistent business behaviors displayed that she felt were subpar, she tackled them head on and tried to change them. Mary also felt there was no need to dumb down her analyses for the salespeople or the members of the larger deal team. She viewed their constant queries as a sign of doubting her capability.

The moral of the story is that it is not enough for a deal team member to be good at the job at hand. A deal team member also needs to be a coach. He or she must not only perform the task at hand but also nurture people to understand the value of the task, articulate the task details simply, and get people on board with the proposition.

Managing Chaos: Guessing What Is Coming up Around the Curve

Not long ago, Anirban was responsible for selling a service-oriented architecture, or SOA-based, solution at IBM. He used a particular YouTube video for his demonstration, which most customers loved. The video was an amazing aerial view of the traffic in Kolkata, India (which happens to be Anirban's birthplace). The video showed the absolute lawlessness of traffic movements—rickshaws, stray cows, and people roaming—along a major street while cars, trucks, public buses, and two-wheelers dash by, with every second portending a potential wreck. It seems like a miracle that nobody gets hurt. What is most remarkable is how everybody seems at peace with the situation. People are chatting on cell phones, driving, and walking around as though it is a normal day. Every time the video was shown, somebody in the room yelled out because they thought they were about to see an accident. But the accident never happened.

Although the point of using the video in customer meetings was to show how IBM tools and services can manage disruptive business behavior, the video also conveyed a broader, and often unnoticed, message. All the people in the scene are comfortable because they are used to it. People learn to drive and walk around successfully while managing to keep themselves together in the middle of disturbing traffic. A deal team member needs to be absolutely comfortable managing deals while being in the middle of utter chaos. We believe there are two important elements to be mastered while managing a pursuit amid chaos.

Showing Emotional Intelligence

According to Wikipedia, *emotional intelligence* (EI) is the ability or skill to perceive, assess, and manage the emotions of oneself, others, and groups.[2] Chaotic times unintentionally bring out the worst in people. Leaders who can bring a sense of security during such periods are much revered. Although crafted strategies and hard-nosed operational drives can help win deals, they are not sufficient to win the hearts and minds of the people affected.

It is extremely important to demonstrate to others that you care for them in this time of need. Does anybody recall how, in the aftermath of September 11, 2001, New York City Mayor Rudolph Giuliani took charge of damage control?[3] He was highly visible, making the rounds at the disaster zone and doing everything he could to rally the city after the attack. He may have made mistakes in his efforts to help, but what was noticeable was that he cared for the people of New York City. They related to him. On the other hand, after Hurricane Katrina hit New Orleans, President George W. Bush received a lot of criticism from across the political spectrum for his rescue efforts. Bush appointed groups from the federal level to help support victims, but his strategic moves were viewed as impersonal and non-caring. If he, and his top leaders, had been more visible in New Orleans—talking to people, giving them a helping hand—he might have won over the hearts of those who were skeptical of his actions.

EI has another dimension: one of hope. President Barack Obama has revived American interest in politics thanks to his message of hope. Whether Obama can deliver on his promises is yet to be seen, but his message of hope invigorates people. What good is a leader who shares your pain and cares for you but cannot show you the perceived path of betterment? Hope can bring significant motivation for the rest of the team to move forward and win deals.

Being a Chess Master

The story in Box 5.5 offers a number of pertinent lessons:

- Don't let the arrogance of others dictate the agenda (clearly this was a factor in the chess match and very nearly worked).
- Never give up; trust your skills and judgment, but give them a chance to breathe.

- Stay the course; take advantage of overconfidence, and do not overlook the power of patience.
- Come with attitude (which is easy to say, but sometimes hard to do).
- Play with character; plan your moves (but move the plan if necessary).
- Finally, close with excellence; win, lose, or draw, play your best game and learn from the results.

Box 5.5: Learning from a School Chess Match

Growing up, Hetzel learned many lessons that have aided his business savvy and entered his experience toolbox. In high school, way back in the early 1970s, when chess enjoyed a high international profile, the annual chess match was revered as the ultimate popularity event. It was not a "brainiac" tournament; star athletes participated to show their mental skills and demonstrate they had more to them than pure brawn. Amazingly enough, the winner two years in a row was the backup quarterback for the varsity football team.

Although the chess match was indeed a test of mental prowess, it was also an obvious test of intimidation and arrogance. Hetzel did well in his initial foray into the contest in his junior year, reaching the semi-finals and a contest with the superstar quarterback, then a senior and vying for his three-in-a-row win to be recorded in school history. The athlete, now only two games away from high school chess immortality, exuded superiority and arrogance. The intimidation was obvious and somewhat successful.

The match was conducted in the school cafeteria with onlookers everywhere (a few hecklers as well as a few well-wishers). Hetzel's opponent was intense in his resolve to win rapidly and without compromise. Within the first 15 minutes of the game, he took Hetzel's queen. It was obvious that within two or three moves checkmate was imminent, but Hetzel regrouped and used every ounce of strategy, including a mid-game time break at the 60-minute mark (when the athlete was obviously growing frustrated that he couldn't get to checkmate), to turn the tables in the mind game. Slowly and methodically, the game shifted momentum with a combination of rook and knight moves that had the now-impatient quarterback pulling out his hair

(continued)

because his own moves were becoming retreats. Just shy of 90 minutes into the game (one of the longest games at that time), the opponent sat in disbelief as his king fell to a checkmate—surrounded by the opposing knight, rook, and one lonely pawn.

Executives love concrete solutions. Business schools teach their students how to break problems into small chunks, dissect them, analyze the bits and pieces, solve the riddle, and finally put the pieces back together. This sounds logical and actually rather scientific. But in the sphere of large deal pursuits the reality is that most of the time you will have only partial information, whereas the deal requires you to understand the complete picture even without essential information. Sometimes you will not have a clue about how much information is needed to really form the complete picture. Experience, expertise, and luck will help you craft the solution. Let's illustrate this with a real-life example, in Box 5.6.

Box 5.6: The Reality of Uncertainty

At the time of writing this book, Satyam was involved in pursuit of a large high-tech deal with a renowned Japanese company. The deal was initially floated as an RFP for a simple infrastructure management support bid that included remote desktop support and server management. It was extremely tempting for the bid team to focus all their energy on getting the proposal camera-ready. From talking to different trusted sources within the organization, we found out that this was one of three large proposals that the company was floating simultaneously. The Indian competitors, the big global brethren and others were already in the fray for the other two RFPs, but not Satyam. To combat this losing proposition (you can't win a deal if you are not invited to bid), the pursuit team made a conscious decision to bypass its IT people and go directly to the business side. SDG championed a campaign and put forward an indicative proposal for combining the three RFPs into one and achieving an overall reduction of cost. Academia would have taught us that we needed to know the

(continued)

details of the other RFPs to really put a good picture together, using a bottom-up approach. In this case, we used our market intelligence and supplemented it with our general outsourcing experience from high-tech industry, to create a compelling story. Uncertainty is reality when leading large deals.

Conclusion

The good thing is that leading from the rear is a learned skill. We hope we have been able to offer some pointers that will help you be more cognizant as you navigate this complex and sometimes treacherous business environment.

Notes

1. Courtney Lynch and Angie Morgan, *Leading from the Front: No-Excuse Leadership Tactics for Women* (New York: McGraw Hill, 2006).
2. See http://en.wikipedia.org/wiki/Emotional_intelligence.
3. Carl W. Stern and Michael S. Deimler (eds.), *The Boston Consulting Group on Strategy: Classic Concepts and New Perspectives,* 2nd ed. (Hoboken, NJ: Wiley, 2006).

CHAPTER 6

Structuring Deals Right

The Art of Pricing

Contrary to what some people in the IT and business-outsourcing industries believe, Big Deals are not dead. Against the backdrop of market-driven demand for Big Deals are some key market observations. First, Big Deals are here to stay and third-party advisors (TPAs) are getting more involved in the process—from simple outsourcing of full-time-equivalent (FTE) to full-blown system integration deals. Second, clients are demanding more flexibility in their contracts by down-sizing from mega deals to more "Big" deals and unbundling services with multiple awards. Also, shorter contract periods are in evidence with a fall to three to seven years, from 10 years, allowing clients to change providers more frequently. This promotes potential redistribution of awards to the broader global service provider base. Finally, the demand for higher-quality, performance-based contracts presents more complex terms with integrated solutions but offers the opportunity for cross-selling services. Figure 6.1 shows some of our current market observations with regard to 2009.

When all is said and done, in deal making pricing or financial creativity is the single most critical part of the solution to the customers in a global sourcing engagement. As much as customers may say that they are buying services because of other intrinsic values, such as improved quality, the harsh reality is that they always care about price. As mentioned in Chapter One, we do not consider pass-through deals as really being Big Deals, regardless of their size. An example of a pass-through deal would be if a service deal had a significant cost for proposed software. The total contract value (TCV) may be high for the deal, but the software maker would actually take the majority of the TCV as the software price.

Unfortunately, as important as pricing is, many service providers still fail to do a thorough pricing analysis. Before you attack this last comment as incorrect, let us explain what it means by using two real-life examples (see Boxes 6.1 and 6.2).

Figure 6.1 Key Market Observations for 2009

Box 6.1: When Pricing Goes Whacky

An RFP came in to a service provider with a short leash. As soon as the bid team was mobilized, they started putting in a zillion hours a day to respond to the RFP. There were cross-continent calls that happened twice every day until the bid went in. A senior bid manager went through the RFP and allocated questions to team members. These team members were held accountable for their inputs. Senior executives were roped in to furnish guidance for the RFP response. Life was good.

But when it came to pricing, things started looking a bit shaky. The various horizontal BUs, who were under tremendous time pressure, came up with some estimates for the work requested. To be safe, all these horizontals plugged in a safe margin on their estimates; so if the work required two FTEs, the horizontals plugged in the need for two and a half FTEs in their estimates. Every horizontal wanted to ensure that its profitability was exceeded, so they all followed similar strategies for offering inputs. The verticals also added some margin for themselves when they supplied their inputs for the work requested. Eventually, all these estimates were aggregated, vetted for a reality check, and then passed on to the finance department to come up with the final pricing. Finance took the hard inputs, baked in corporate norms (read: profitability), and came up with the final pricing.

(continued)

The lead salesperson in the bid team knew the drill. As soon, as the pricing came in, she lobbied hard with senior BU leaders to work with finance and corporate to reduce the quote. After much deliberation and discussion, the quote was lowered significantly and the bid was turned in.

The bid team's joy about work well done was short-lived when they found out that another provider had swept the deal away from them by submitting a more aggressive price. The deal team wondered long and hard about how they had lost the deal, when they gave significant discounts and priced it just as the customer asked.

Box 6.2: Looking Beyond What Is Easily Visible

We have met several TPAs who told us that they find it difficult to evaluate one particular large global service provider. Typically, TPAs like to create an environment where they can set benchmarks and metrics so that all service providers bidding for a job can be compared to each other as apples to apples. Well, some TPAs dislike this service provider because this company does not simply answer the questions asked by the TPA. It almost always gives a compelling business case that shows an attractive total cost of ownership (TCO) reduction for the customer using "various means." A lot of those various means were not those that the customer asked for in the RFP (such options may include alternate pricing or asset discounts). The service provider in question may also give exactly what the TPA asked for in the desired format but the extra documentation, showing the business benefits and overall cost reduction proposition, definitely tempts the customer into wanting to continue dialogue with this provider. Lo and behold, very soon the TPA gets sidelined and the provider makes the services sale along with the software, hardware, and other ancillary items.

The two stories depicted in Boxes 6.1 and 6.2 represent polar opposites. We have seen variations of the first story play out way too many times at numerous provider organizations. Experienced deal makers can vouch for this type of story. The first impression here may be that the bid was lost because estimations were incorrect. Too much profit was sneaked in at different places and the total discount applied did not offset the unnecessary padding. Although this analysis is 100 percent true, we believe that the root cause of the problem was much deeper. The provider failed to properly understand the customer and its drivers for outsourcing. The provider primarily focused on responding to the RFP only and looked at pricing as one part of the RFP. The second story depicts a provider that really understood the pulse of the customer. This provider went beyond what was asked in the RFP and offered solutions that were not even part of the equation.

The lesson learned here is that pricing cannot be viewed as a stand-alone part of the RFP. Pricing is really a subset of the commercial model. In our minds, the commercial model is a combination of the sourcing model, the engagement model, and the pricing model. The sourcing model should support the engagement model, which in turn supports the pricing model—and all three are wrapped together in creative commercial terms and conditions. We would be remiss without mentioning the expertise required to engage in this holistic pricing process. A delicate balance between true CFO accounting discipline and creative strategic financial models is the recipe for closing large and profitable deals. There is no worse deed done than to close a bad deal. Clearly, there is a conflict here between Chapter Four (keeping the TPAs in good stead) and what we are advocating through this holistic model (which TPAs may not, unless championed by them, as we pointed out). Unfortunately there is no straight answer on how one can walk that fine line. The deal team members, TPA relationship manager, and senior executives of the service provider all tap into their networks within the assigned TPA and the customer base to pacify folks and reduce anger. Our recommendation is that even if you prescribe a holistic solution that is not exactly what the TPA originally wanted, ensure that you work with the TPA to place the proposal in front of the customer such that the TPA's position is not undermined.

What's Your Customer's Sourcing Model?

Pricing preparation should start as soon as the RFP (or RFI) comes in. Pricing technology services offerings is very different from pricing product offerings. Here, the quote is completely intertwined with the solution estimate. The biggest mistake a provider makes on getting an

RFP is to start immediately answering the questions in it. We believe in a three-step sourcing-model analysis process for all Big Deals.

1. *Read the RFP* As soon as the RFP comes in, all the core team members should read it in entirety. As trivial as this sounds, most of the time not all the core team members read the whole RFP. People tend to zone in on the bits and pieces relevant to themselves.

2. *Analyze the provider wish list* It is extremely valuable to know what you want out of the deal. You may have to change your "want" position as you go further down the deal, but it is important to have this as a start. Many bid teams use a four-step due process in this segment. First, sourcing strategy is defined, followed by sourcing initiation and then enhancement; finally, sourcing governance is put in place. Once the bid team has been through a series of questions (as defined in Figure 6.2), they will have a good understanding about what they want to achieve from this deal as a service provider. So the provider wish list analysis needs to be a group exercise

1. Sourcing Strategy	**2. Sourcing Initiative**
What do we want to **achieve**? How to determine **costs, benefits**, and **risks**? How to baseline **current performance** and **costs**? What is the **risk-optimal sourcing strategy**? What is the **best governance structure**? What **engagement models** should we employ?	How to develop **accurate sourcing requirements**? How to select the **right partners**? How to equip people to **negotiate effectively**? How to **manage risks**?

3. Sourcing Governance	**4. Sourcing Enhancement**
How to proactively **manage relationships**? How to **define metrics** for monitoring partners? How to **structure governance framework**? How to **manage change**? How to **resolve disputes**?	How to **ensure all objectives are met**? How to **assess** sourcing performance? How to **continuously improve programs**? How to **pursue improvement goals**?

Figure 6.2 A Recommended Four-Step Process for Analyzing the Deal Wish List

among senior people from the BU and the deals group. This discussion should happen face-to-face if possible. Obviously, when you are discussing these answers, you need to bounce the ideas off the RFP to ensure that you are not completely off-track. For example, if the RFP asked for all work to be done onsite and you present an engagement model that is highly offshore-centric, then you are simply wasting time. But pushing the envelope is OK. If the customer asked for offshore quotes from Malaysia, don't hesitate to show China quotes as an alternative.

3. *Understand customer sourcing tolerance* Understanding a customer's sourcing tolerance stems from the amount of intelligence you have about the customer. Your account team members for this customer should give you information on the customer's psychology. Take the time to understand the preferred or tolerated sourcing model of the customer. Is your customer the type that believes they can do it all in a cost-effective way and do not need a provider? Or are they the type that believes the provider can do it all? Most large customers fall somewhere in the middle, where they want to share the work with the provider. Figure 6.3 simplifies global sourcing models from a customer's perspective. Once you have an idea of the global sourcing preference of the customer, it's time to verify again if that sourcing model can support what you want on

Figure 6.3 Global Sourcing Models from a Customer Perspective

the basis of the findings on the wish list of your organization. If the answer is yes, or if you can create a negotiated position that works for you, go forward with creating the engagement model for the customer.

Big Deal Engagement Models: Laying the Bed for Pricing

Before creating an engagement model or a combination of various engagement models, it is essential to realize that there is no right or wrong solution. The model should be chosen according to a combination of business drivers applicable for a customer or a particular business within a customer. You can expand this list of drivers as much as you would like:

- *Business need* What is the customer trying to achieve?
- *Cost of ownership* What is their TCO if the customer does it alone? What is the management or support overhead for this deal?
- *Security* Does the customer feel that providers using a global sourcing model can provide the necessary security?
- *Risk and reward* What is the customer's risk if the customer does not do the engagement? On the flip side, if the work is done right, what is gained? Can we quantify the gain or loss in monetary terms?
- *Process maturity* How matured is their existing delivery process? How does it compare to industry benchmarks and their peers?
- *Engagement duration* What is the duration of the deal?
- *Competencies* What skill sets (both technical and functional) will be needed to support this deal?
- *Costs* How much will it cost us, as a provider, to do the work?
- *Size* What is the size of the deal in monetary terms?
- *Scalability* Does the solution need to be scaled? If so, to what extent?
- *Time to market* Is the solution that we are building for the customer going to help deliver the end product to its own customers faster?
- *Business application* Is this deal going to support the customer's core application or non-core applications?

The answers from these questions should give you enough ammunition to suggest engagement models not defined in the RFP. Think about the anecdote in Box 6.2, where the provider always gave something extra. To make pricing effective and attractive, it is vital to base it on the right engagement model.

Here is a summary of the most common Big Deal engagement models.

Staff Augmentation

In the early days of Big Deals, the engagement models were mostly based on skill or staff augmentation (also called "body shopping"). The concept was a fairly simple, procurement-based process. You have resources, they cost a certain amount, and your customer is going to hire those resources from you and pay you by the hour. You may give some volume discount based on total resources hired. The customer is responsible for resource planning, managing those resources, and having the resources do the work. This is primarily a transaction-based approach. There is no long-term commitment between the customer and the provider. RFPs are typically issued for every project. The service providers are not supposed to invest in items such as infra-structure, assets, and knowledge transfer. Service providers are also not involved in technology and strategy planning. Generally, the service providers lean on the customers to create a risk-mitigation strategy for the projects and programs. In this model, the customer would use some of the value of global sourcing benefits, but not that much.

Managed Services

A few years back, large service-delivery providers started moving into a managed services model. In this model, the service providers were actually responsible for delivering the customer's outcomes. This model requires the customer and the service provider to work closely together. It also forces the service provider to truly understand the customer's requirements and risks. It is almost impossible to win a deal with this model unless risk mitigation can be demonstrated. If done well, the global sourcing value provided to the customer is much greater with this model than with the old skill augmentation model. Service providers are also expected to invest in infrastructure and furnish their knowledge base to the customer to help joint planning. This model thrives on the belief that service providers become long-term strategic allies for the customer.

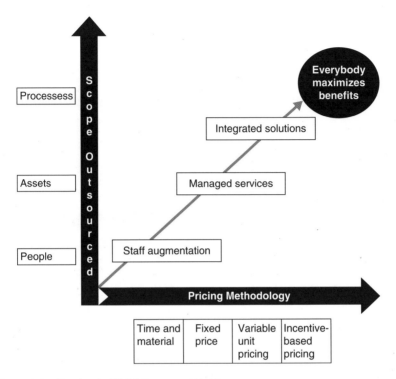

Figure 6.4 Choosing the "Right" Engagement Models

Integrated Solutions

The integrated solutions model is a step beyond the managed services model and affords the most global sourcing value to the customer. We believe the future of large deals is integrated solutions. Here, the service providers own the customer outcome and are not just responsible for delivering it. Just like managed services, service providers using an integrated solutions model are expected to invest in infrastructure and provide their knowledge base to the customer to help joint planning. Service providers are also expected to make process improvements here as well as critical strategy decisions for the customer. We are still in the infancy of this model.

Figures 6.4 and 6.5 show the journey of a large-deal engagement model.

It is important to remember that this is not a zero-sum game. All three engagement models, or variations of them, can be applied for the same customer. Once there is clarity about the engagement models, it is time to price the deal.

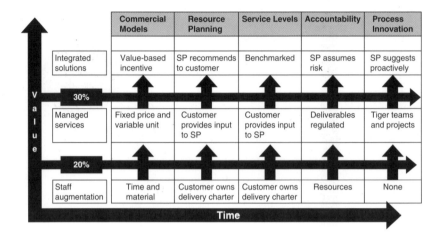

	Commercial Models	Resource Planning	Service Levels	Accountability	Process Innovation
Integrated solutions	Value-based incentive	SP recommends to customer	Benchmarked	SP assumes risk	SP suggests proactively
30%					
Managed services	Fixed price and variable unit	Customer provides input to SP	Customer provides input to SP	Deliverables regulated	Tiger teams and projects
20%					
Staff augmentation	Time and material	Customer owns delivery charter	Customer owns delivery charter	Resources	None

Figure 6.5 Engagement Model Based on Customer Business Drivers

The Price Is Right! What Customers Want

We believe that any type of commercial model could be used within any of the three engagement models described here. Although we will cover, in some detail, the pluses and minuses for each type of pricing model, the focus is really on how you drive these models.

Here are some of our recommended guidelines for Big Deals pricing. These fundamentals should be kept in mind regardless of the pricing model you are choosing.

- *Margin* For Big Deals, the total margins should be greater than or equal to historical company norms over the life of the deal. However, this measure is not set in stone. For specific deals that are extremely strategic (such as achieving openings in new industries), service providers should consider dropping margins to win the deals.
- *Cash flow* The goal should be to achieve positive cash flow annually. You may choose negative cash flow in year one if it is a multi-year deal.
- *Overhead* Incremental overhead should be factored in as part of the pricing algorithm.
- *Foreign exchange (FX) fluctuation* In today's world of currency volatility, it is crucial to factor in the effects and mitigation strategies for foreign exchange fluctuation in the pricing model.
- *Cost of living adjustment (COLA)* An accurate COLA should be part of all large-deal pricing.

- *Taxes* For most large deals, the customer should pay service taxes and right-to-use consents.
- *Transition costs* Transition costs should be paid up front by the customer or amortized with termination charges. Don't be surprised, though, if the customer wants free transition-planning estimates, based on due diligence, during contract negotiation. Creating the estimates will require investment in person-hours. We are seeing some TPAs corner service providers into this commitment.
- *Productivity* There should be a minimum of 3 percent productivity per year built into the deal.
- *Duration* A Big Deal should be for a minimum three-year term, but we prefer seven-to-10-year deals.
- *Human resource (HR) assets* Assume HR assets (people) from the customer at customer costs.
- *Equipment assets* Assume responsibility for the complete acquisition of equipment. This also includes assuming responsibility for asset refreshment only in terms of a service fee, without taking full ownership.

Along with the pricing fundamentals noted here, it is also imperative to get a grip on the levers that will help you manage your costs and ultimately the deal.

- *Billing rates* You need to keep your billing rates competitive. Chapter Eight covers some of the ploys that customers or TPAs use to reduce your rates, based on some phony benchmarks. You need to be aware of these practices and be firm on rates to a certain degree.
- *Cost of delivery* Efforts should be made to keep the cost of delivery low. This practice should apply not just for onsite resources but for all offshore locations as well. Financial models should force service providers to create repeatable delivery mechanisms to cut down costs on learning and transitions. An example would be using a rational unified process (RUP) to do delivery work so that economies of scale can be achieved when scaled. Also, service providers should always focus on reducing sales, general, and administrative (SG&A) expenses.
- *Cross-sell and up-sell* The pricing models should assume some year-to-year growth based on cross-sell and up-sell in the account. This assumption keeps the sales team and account teams motivated to grow within the account.

This pricing best practice section wouldn't be complete without a word about curtailing greed (See Box 6.3).

Box 6.3: A Small Lesson on Greed

Anirban learned a harsh lesson on curtailing greed early when he was growing up in India. This lesson has helped him tremendously in his sales career. Anirban's family help had a pet goat (yes, you read it right). This goat had an eating disorder; it simply could not contain itself and always kept eating. Neighborhood babies in strollers and kids on bikes used to make the rounds to see the ultrafat goat.

One morning, Anirban woke up in the midst of hearing some crying, only to realize that the goat's stomach had exploded. The goat died through overfeeding himself. Although it was a gory sight, the lesson that came with it was enough of a reminder for the eight-year-old boy to understand how greed can be self-destructive. We all saw the goat reemerge when Wall Street recently burst thanks to uncontrolled corporate greed coupled with an appetite for risky ventures.

The story about greed has much relevance to global sourcing bids. In the anecdote in Box 6.1, the service provider's bids were bloated because every horizontal and corporate kept adding margins without realizing the consequences. The greed for higher numbers can actually kill the deal, as it did in that story. Margins are healthy, but it's an absolute must to be reasonable when adding margins. Sometimes, it is not greed but uncertainty that factors into padded estimates. Every BU thinks, "I don't want to be late; I'm not exactly sure how long this work will take, so let me add some margin to my best guess." Many deal makers handle this situation by arbitrarily lowering numbers across the board before submitting a bid. We do not recommend this approach because you can actually jeopardize delivery by penalizing a group that produced accurate and reasonable estimates. Instead, we recommend that you as a deal maker talk to every BU individually and negotiate the estimates. The process can be time-consuming and frustrating (you are operating under a tight deadline) but necessary. If you are really keen on making this estimating process better, here is a suggestion. Study old bids and compare original estimates with actual.

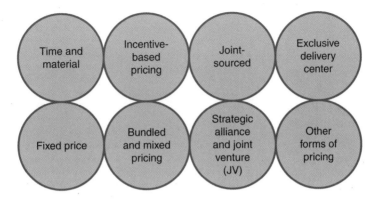

Figure 6.6 Pricing Models

Although delivery work changes a lot from the time the deal was actually signed, you can still get a fairly good understanding of which group uses the most padding. This data will give you added leverage when you are negotiating estimates with the BUs. Don't be surprised, though, if you cannot find the data. Snooping around in past deals to find this type of information is generally frowned on by BU lead delivery teams and greeted with obstruction.

There are many pricing models used for Big Deals. For the sake of this book, we will focus on the ones we have seen work best in such circumstances. If you look at Figure 6.6, you will see a total of eight Big Deal pricing models. "Incentive-based," "joint-sourced," and "strategic alliance and joint venture (JV)" are advanced pricing models; we will discuss them in greater depth in Chapter Seven. In this chapter, we give you our take on the other pricing models:

- Fixed price
- Time and material (T&M)
- Bundled and mixed pricing
- Exclusive delivery center
- Other models

Fixed Price (Fixed Bid)

We believe that if you have confidence in engagement scoping and deliverables, you should recommend this model to your customers. Simply put, customers pay a fixed price for services received. How you do it as a service provider is up to you for the most part. Customers, however, do like to see and approve the plans regarding the onsite-offshore mix.

Today, we believe that about a third of large deals are fixed bids. Most service providers, using managed services and integrated services engagement models, are big proponents of using fixed bid as a pricing tool.

Customers benefit from the service provider's reusability of design and deployment of best practices. Fixed bids tend to improve customer initiatives such as increasing time to market, managing costs, and operating expenses. The customers get an assurance of risk since they know the total cost. You can also cover your base as a service provider by negotiating hard on the deliverables and milestones. You can even extend this model to reflect price based on outputs, sometimes called output-based pricing.

We have run into some TPAs and customers who resist this model. Their main fear is that the scope is not understood by the service provider. Also, fixed-bid contracts tend to be very detailed and complex, which customers hate. A major problem arises when change happens. If customers change course frequently, service providers add change request (CR) fees, which make the price grow steep. We know many customers who went with big global service providers, got a great fixed-bid deal, and then lost their pants because of CR costs. As a service provider who really wants to engage in a win-win relationship with your customer, you need to discuss how to handle change with your customer from the outset of the deal.

Time and Material (T&M)

T&M is the oldest of Big Deal pricing models. It is primarily an effort-based billing exercise. The connectivity, associated hardware, and software costs are borne by the customer. Service providers charge rates that are dependent on expertise, experience, location, and the duration of the work. The skill augmentation engagement model mainly uses T&M pricing.

Although we are not great fans of the traditional T&M model, it has its pluses. This model is good if the customer and the service provider do not understand the scope of work or if the scope is evolving. T&M can also be used for the repetitive type of support roles where volume fluctuates and is also a key driver (for example, in business-process outsourcing or BPO). Typically, T&M models assume that offshore resources work 45 hours a week as opposed to 40, which is the U.S. standard, greater output can be achieved.

T&M sure has its drawbacks as well. Overall knowledge retention is hard for the service provider and the customer. The billable resources operate almost like a revolving door, coming in and going out. Because service providers are less accountable, it is impossible for them to take center stage, build a relationship, and truly add value. Service providers also tend to get blamed for cost overruns because the customer feels the resources supplied by the service provider were not at par, which resulted in more person-hours required for a job that should have taken less time. In reality, customers often fail to manage projects and tend to blame the results on service providers. Service providers also fail to add any process, tools, or best practice improvements because they are really only order takers under this model.

For service providers, T&M is a definitely a way to get your foot in the door. But the goal should be to move on to more challenging models and add far more value for the customer.

Surprisingly enough, as service providers we prefer a variation of T&M called "T&M with cap." In this model, there is a limit on how much the service provider can charge. We believe that T&M with cap builds collaboration and trust between the customer and the service provider—ingredients that are the cornerstones of any successful business structure. We have also used T&M models that include reward metrics where both customer and service provider share costs saved. This model requires transparency from both sides. We discuss this gain-sharing concept in Chapter Seven.

Bundled and Mixed Pricing

The bundled concept combines pricing for offshore plus onsite along with a variety of skills. The mixed pricing allows customers to choose between T&M and fixed price. Customers like this because they get a single rate. The service provider's processes, tools, and best practices can be applied to this model. This model is still picking up steam because it requires a thorough understanding of the deal from both buyers and service providers, which does not happen often. Also, the contracts supporting this model can be brutally detailed. We think that as customers and service providers grow comfortable with the integrated solutions engagement model, we will start seeing more of this type of pricing along with it.

Exclusive Delivery Center

In this model, service providers dedicate a facility that is exclusive to a single customer. This center, generally hosted offshore, actually replicates a customer's environment. Service provider employees working for a particular customer are the only people who can enter the highly secured area.

Service providers can give higher benefits to customers and retain resources and knowledge because they control the projects. Customers also have greater control because they can appraise the service provider's staff. This model also makes the customer feel at ease, especially if the service provider is dealing with the customer's prized intellectual property (IP).

This model requires significant attention and investment, so the service provider and the customer need to be sure that a large workload will be sustainable for a legitimate duration of at least three to five years to make the return on investment (ROI) work for the customer.

Other Models

There are a variety of other pricing models that service providers can use in order to win a Big Deal. One such common approach is called *rebadge*. In simple terms, service providers take over customer employees (and sometimes even other contractors who have a deal with the customer). Typically, the initial base case is a cost-plus model. Sometimes, customers find rebadging useful because it helps them gracefully let go of employees working in areas where they do not want to focus. It also assures the customer that transition and operations will continue without major problems because the people already know the work and environment. Service providers pondering this approach need to think beyond the short run. If you feel you can use these resources beyond their current engagement, then they are a good asset. However, if these resources work in areas where you are not focused, then it may do no good to obtain them. Generally, a service provider matches the existing benefits that the rebadged employees were receiving at the customer. You have to pay special attention to the employment benefits and retirement benefits that these rebadged employees are entitled to and factor them into your cost model.

Another fixed-bid type of model uses the concept of *total cost of ownership (TCO) reduction* for the customer. Here, the service provider analyzes what the customer spends and promises a percentage saving. Service providers sometimes struggle to attain profitability with this model if the duration of the engagement is less than five years. Also, like fixed bids, service providers need to be assured that the scope is well understood.

A few years back, the IT outsourcing industry was buzzing about *utility-based pricing* in the context of broader infrastructure services. The idea was to share more resource units (computer processors, servers, desktops) among users, thereby charging the buyer only for real usage. This translated to lower overall costs for the buyer. It also represented a real opportunity for outsourcing service providers, who could be the aggregators of the service and then allocate it out to multiple customers, creating a win-win for all parties involved. Server consolidations went from a reduction in the number of "boxes" to "partitions" (multiple users per box). A further breakdown of costs (which included hardware, software, and service costs divided into total cost units) was made possible by software programs running on newer hardware platforms and capturing all the cost elements for reliable pricing. The big outsourcing deal between IBM and AMEX in 2002 (US$4 billion) showcased utility pricing and was followed by EDS and HP closing mega outsourcing deals that were also based on the utility model.

Virtualization is in fact the next big differentiator for infrastructure pricing. It is the panacea, and as history has proven, it is possible, but there is still much work to be done. There is no question in our minds that the service providers who can offer the buyer creative, reliable, and predictable pricing that has ultimate flexibility in scaling up and down with usage based on the ultimate demand of their end user will grab outsourcing market share. After all, what buyer wouldn't stand in line to buy this offering? The question is which service providers will present models that adequately share the risks to allow this to be sustainable for all parties. We don't see this being routinely offered for at least a couple of years—but hey, keep your mind and eyes open!

Conclusion: Risk Mitigation, Customer Focus, and Relationships Are All That Matters

It is easy to get lost in all the sourcing models, engagement models, and pricing models discussed in this chapter. The key takeaway is that whatever model you are prescribing should achieve three things:

it should (1) make your customer feel safe; (2) help the customer achieve its business objectives; and (3) leave you open to discussing and changing the model if needed, on the basis of your open relationship with the customer.

Our experience has taught us that negotiating commercial propositions is harder internally than externally. Many bid teams grow frustrated because they cannot get corporate finance to agree to sign off on a certain model or price. We recommend bid team members make corporate finance a part of their team. There is no better team than those who work and play together. Typically, the financial strategists understand business impacts and corporate finance understands detailed accounting obligations, so they can communicate successfully on your behalf, both internally and externally with your customers.

CHAPTER 7

Advanced Deal Structuring

Creating Innovative Engagement Models and Being Customer Financiers

In Chapter Six, we went into some depth on creating the right pricing. We would like to believe that pricing a solution right will help us win business. Our experience tells us, however, that if you offer simple pricing, you will be used as a benchmark to compare other bids, but you probably won't win. We have fallen victim to that many times in our deal-making careers.

Big Deals require innovative pricing models. Global sourcing customers expect service providers to offer some form of pricing that encourages the service providers to invest in the deal as well. Tech Mahindra, a global sourcing player with a niche, made headlines in early 2008 by winning a Big Deal from British Telecom (BT). The deal was unique at that time because Tech Mahindra paid US$100 million up front as part of future savings to clinch the deal. But that situation is not unique anymore. Many large IT outsourcing customers are demanding hefty up-front savings payment from service providers to tide over the global slowdown and credit squeeze. "One large insurance company, currently discussing a contract, demands over US$100 million upfront payment as part of the savings promised by a vendor," said a top executive of a leading tech firm who did not wish to be named.[1] Service providers must be creative in deal structuring in order to support such heavy investments in customers.

Our advice would be to put in some innovative deal structuring with every bid, even if your customer asks for a simple rate card. Service providers also need to use creative structuring so that they do not fall victim to a price war. It is always an art to set the right margin targets. We believe there needs to be a "reasonable" margin if long-term growth is to be sustained. We used the word *reasonable* here because there is really no clear definition of what a margin should be for a Big Deal. We have seen Big Deals carry margins anywhere from 5 percent to 45 percent of earned revenue. Reasonable margin should be set on the basis of assessing market realities (economic condition, customer's business condition, and so on), desperation to win the deal, and last but not least, consensus on a margin percentage. That third point is critical because corporate finance, business unit leaders from the involved business units, and deal group leaders need to agree on the margin before building the proposed price.

To make innovative pricing effective, service providers have to understand customer cost structure. Even if you cannot get the data yourself, you must go to a TPA or an industry analyst firm, such as Gartner or Forrester, to get benchmark data. You should understand where your base costs lie compared to your customers. Innovative pricing also brings in new business models, which can help the customer with process innovation. In the rest of this chapter, we address some innovative models:

- Incentive-based or gain-sharing model
- Joint-sourced model
- Strategic alliance model or joint venture (JV)

Incentive-Based or Gain-Sharing Model: The Carrot-and-Stick Approach

One such popular pricing model for Big Deals is incentive-based pricing. Colloquially, deal makers say it is the carrot-and-stick model. Most of the incentives are designed to yield continuous benefits for the customer. In the early years, the global sourcing industry made a clear distinction between incentive-based models and gain-sharing models. Incentives were designed only to reward service providers, but gain-sharing had both reward and disincentive components, thereby helping customers and service providers. Gradually, we have seen these models merge to a point where they are interchangeably called incentive-based or gain-sharing models.

However, some customers feel that we service providers can somehow magically con our way around metrics into getting greater rewards. Customers generally force service providers to put a cap on their incentives. Instead of simply agreeing to a cap-on-incentives approach, we favor a different one. Why not bargain for getting the most rewards but base it on customer savings? Let's demonstrate this with a real-life example (see Box 7.1).

Box 7.1: The Woes of Risk and Reward: A Lesson Learned

A few years back, Anirban was representing a well-known customer in a large global sourcing deal. The TCV was more than US$100 million. The customer was third in its space, and eager to increase its market share but wary about the whole concept of global sourcing. The reason was that the customer did not have much experience in managing globally distributed service delivery. Most of the managers and directors had worked at the customer company for a long time and were quite set in their ways.

This customer hired one of the top TPAs to negotiate the deal. The TPA was given clear instruction to ensure that the service provider could not trick the customer by securing undue rewards. It was a hard sell. Finally, the deal was sealed with the following terms. It was fixed-bid contract for five years. The customer could cancel the contract at any time with minimum penalty. The risk-reward ratio could be triggered in a number of ways; cost savings was one of them. The service provider, in this case, was planning to save 35 percent of the customer's current spending in year one and 65 percent of spending over five years. If the service provider beat those expectations, it would get 15 percent of the savings; if the service provider failed to produce the benefits, it would pay a maximum of 10 percent penalty on the expenditure. If it simply met the targets, no bonus was paid. The bonus would be calculated annually on the basis of yearly measures.

The first year turned out to be a disaster for all. The service provider actually missed the targets, and the customer had to fight the service provider for the penalties. A thorough analysis showed the reason. The service provider assumed it was going to be able to get temporary resources from India to relocate onsite and do proper intakes of knowledge transfer (KT). The service provider, however, did not factor in one simple measure: the time taken for these offshore-based employees to obtain U.S. visas. In year one of the contract, the waiting period for a U.S. visa interview, across all U.S. consulates in India, was several months. Previously, it would only have taken a couple of weeks. The

(continued)

reason was the sudden increase in security alerts in response to the threat of terrorist activity. The resource crunch disturbed the KT process and proper turnover. The service provider opted to use less-experienced U.S.-based employees to fill the shoes of experienced Indian workers. The less-experienced U.S.-based employees were used to save money. But their lack of technology skills hurt the service provider tremendously. By the end of the year, quite a few service level agreements (SLAs) had been missed and the customer's business requirements were hampered. The customer, who already had an anti-sourcing community within the organization, was up in arms, and there were many who wanted to get the service provider out. That outcry resulted in nothing more concrete than griping remarks because the customer had to outsource its work in order to stay in business.

This story has a happy ending, though. The service provider turned things around from year two onward. They had to renegotiate part of the contract and hire more subject matter experts from the customer to get the deal going. The service provider started exceeding targets by year three. The deal was a lesson learned for both the customer and the service provider.

Although the story in the box may make you think it is not wise to go into a reward-sharing agreement, it can actually be quite profitable if done right. You just need to ensure that certain best practices are followed. The next sections describe some best practices that we believe in.

Align Risks and Gains to Incentives and Penalties

When writing contracts, the focus should be on structuring the deal in such a way that the rewards and penalties are directly aligned to customer objectives. If the customer wants to improve resolution time for severity one tickets, the incentives and disincentives should be based on doing so. But this needs to be realistic in nature. Although it might be tempting to bet the farm—that is to say, take big risks in the hope of getting handsomely rewarded, but also face the heavy consequences of failure—you are best advised to adopt a moderate strategy. For example, if the customer is adamant that you resolve all severity one tickets within 15 minutes, you need to find out what happens if the time is delayed. How much does the customer lose for delays to resolution? Once this is established, you can work out a disincentive plan. You should never agree to accept the entire liability. Similarly, if you beat resolution times, you need to work out an acceptable reward. The best way to align gains and disincentives is to tie them directly to the customer's business performance. An example of this is when a particular service provider works with some energy and utility (E&U) customers. The gain-sharing strategy is aligned to common industry E&U metrics: earnings per share (EPS) and cost per kilowatt-hour. In this way, the customer executives and this service provider are aligned linearly on gains. There is motivation on both sides to do the right thing. Although one may question the practicality of tying the customer's end business performance with that of the service provider, in a true collaborative model the service provider and the customer should agree on the metrics. After all, the goal of the customer is to improve its business performance.

Objectivity Prevails (Almost)

The key here is to establish the measures objectively and quantifiably. They must never be subjective. If you fall into that trap, customer middle management will always kill you with complaints. Our recommendation is never to base an incentive clause on subjective customer satisfaction. However, objective models cannot be rigid mathematical contracts either. There needs to be an element of "normalization" involved. Quarterly or monthly strategic meetings will resolve what element of rewards or penalties can be applied for specific outcomes. Collaboration is the key to creating the measures.

Balance Duration and Incentives

Customers often tend to furnish incentives that are based on long-term or short-term goals but don't balance them as a pair. Let us illustrate this with an example. Suppose you, as a service provider, signed up to do some innovation for the customer. Now, to innovate, you might have to tweak things a little bit. The tweaking may lead to some deviations in the original customer-defined metrics. If you are punished for all of these infractions, you will focus only on short-term target achievements. Then you will miss the long-term innovation target. By the same token, short-term actions should also have rewards and consequences.

Service providers must work with customers to align incentives according to both short-term and long-term outcomes.

To summarize: in any incentive-based pricing the service provider incentives have to be tied with direct customer benefits. The pricing does not necessarily have to be cost-driven; it can be market-driven as well. Collaboration with the customer will result in the ultimate win-win model.

Joint-Sourced Models: A Perfect Marriage

It is a pity that we have not seen massive use of joint-sourced models in the industry yet. Some service providers call it the co-sourcing model. The joint-sourced model is the ultimate result-oriented partnership between the customer and the service provider. In an ideal world, the customer and the service provider would allow total and complete visibility of one another's cost bases, operational models, and customer business objectives. The service provider gets paid using a dual scheme. The first part is the cost factor, where it receives payments for incurred costs and overheads. The second part is the plus factor, where it receives profit. The profit is dependent on meeting customer metrics. The customer knows the service provider's profit percentage, which is agreed by both parties (we are all in it to make money). We recommend service providers structure this model in such a way that the cost factor also carries a small profit built in within the overhead factors. You are thereby at least partially covered against the downside.

If this model sounds like an incentive-based or gain-sharing model, that's because it is. The two big differentiators between this model and the incentive-based model are that in this case (1) both the customer and the service provider are allowed to see the other's operation, and (2) they have mutual trust. For this model to work successfully, we believe that three key areas of collaboration need to be established. The customer-service provider partnership should be reflected in strategy, process, and information management.

Strategy

The service provider has to be deeply involved in understanding the customer's business strategy. The sourcing plan must be developed jointly between the customer and the service provider. If a TPA is assisting the customer, the customer needs to ensure that the TPA is giving the service provider free access to all information.

Process

The operational processes that will drive performance metrics should be jointly developed by the service provider and the customer.

Information Management

Because the customer has clear visibility of our resource-loading factors, cost models, full-term-equivalent (FTE) rates, and operations structure, their people can effectively manage provider resources both onsite and offshore. They already have the advantage of knowing their business. In the best-case scenario, customers can actually work with providers to create the most efficient model for them. This collaboration can also eliminate a lot of duplicate process, project, and program managers from the service provider side. Sure, there will be people needed to manage the cultural divide, but massive inefficiencies can be reduced, driving down time and costs.

The joint-sourced model advocates opening solution and pricing models to our customer, soliciting their help in building the operational structure, and having them take a more direct role in managing service provider resources. We believe that for this model to work well, a strong executive-level relationship has to be established between the service provider and the customer. Also, the CIO office, or the head of sourcing in the customer community, should have enough clout to destroy any mutiny in the customer organization that can dampen service provider power. We have seen employees from both sides (customer and service provider) wanting to swap roles, or pursue voluntary job changes with the other company. Typically, these employee-driven initiatives are all championed from the operations level up. But for all these benefits to materialize, this model should operate for at least five to seven years.

This model is also changing for the better. We interviewed Nirmal (Nimma) Bakshi to understand how he envisions future joint-sourcing models. Although Nimma's day job is defining alliance strategies for a major IT services provider, he is a profound thinker who likes to toy with futuristic sourcing models. We vetted what we had learned from

Nimma with several BU leaders at other service providers. We found that the joint-sourcing model is evolving into one that goes beyond technology, domain, and sourcing boundaries where the customer and the service provider can co-source an outcome-based optimized deal. What does this mean?

Today, vertical BUs tend to offer solutions to their customers. These units wrap domain-centric solutions around their technology service offerings and price them in a number of ways. Sometimes deals are simply structured around technology towers. For example, customers may want application maintenance solutions along with some infrastructure management solutions. But in all cases, deals structured today are based on fairly specific customer requirements.

However, in today's efficiency-craving market, many deals are no longer driven by domain-specific solution towers. You can be assured that the deals are not being driven by technology towers either. Instead, deals are driven by broader operational outcomes. Customers are giving service providers broader but accurate business targets. For example, we envision a drastic reduction in the number of RFPs coming from customers. RFPs are being be replaced by problem statements. Don't be surprised if you see a major network switch service provider (customer) coming up with a broad statement such as "We want our global sourcing service provider to help us take away 30 percent market share from our nearest competitor within five years." Do you really believe you can be successful in winning that deal by keeping the vertical and horizontal lines of your business structure in mind? We think not!

As the service providers move away from responding to RFPs and RFIs, the biggest challenge will be to act like a business owner while doing work for a customer. The service provider needs to analyze the customer-given problem statement and make its own assessment. Does solving the customer-given problem really help the customer in the long run? Will it help the customer go beyond achieving marginal gains? Are there areas that the customer needs to focus on to derive a market advantage? Should the customer go into other areas of business that it is not currently focused on? These questions seem like the ones asked by management consultants. Now, as service providers, it is our responsibility to find the answers to these questions and make our analysis based on market knowledge. We cannot operationally drive success if strategic flow-through is absent.

The same vetting processes apply to selecting operational strategies. Because the solution will be a true mix of best-of-breed domain and technical competencies spanning the verticals and horizontals resources will need to come from all sectors. Deal makers will have to lean not only on the traditional BUs but also on the support units, such as marketing, advertising, and other peripheral businesses, to make the customer successful. Remember, you are helping with a solution for the broader problem statement and not simply responding to a defined RFP. It is crucial to have a good understanding of the quality of the varied resource pool and their availability to work on the current pursuit. But before agreeing to work deals, market demands need to be kept in mind. What will you do, as a business leader, with all these resources once your project is over? Does the market have enough traction to use these people? The appropriate resource-mix response to market volatility needs to be kept in mind when applying resources to these deals. The same method will prevail in selecting or deselecting existing customer technology. Does it make sense to continue using Java-based solutions for this customer? How will it affect the customer's business five years from now?

The end goal should be that after your analysis you will have a clear solution model that actually creates or verifies a business strategy and, more important, translates it into clear operational objectives.

Strategic Alliance Models and Joint Ventures: Like Working with Friends and Neighbors

In the sourcing industry, the term *alliance* sometimes confuses people. When we service providers talk about alliances, customers think in terms of product alliances. For example, most of the major service providers have alliances with several hundred product and application companies. These companies create a service around these products and sometimes even resell them. Service providers are more comfortable negotiating license-sale revenues with alliances and original equipment manufacturers (OEMs) than focusing on how to align multiple OEMs and partners to drive customer solutions. Today, it's true that we, as service providers, use partners and alliances to help customers by uniting in a prime-sub relationship. But do we really reach the point where we are using alliances as an integral part of deals? For example, how many times do we preach building a center of excellence that incorporates our solutions along with those of our multiple alliances? Or when we use other service providers as subs, do we, as the prime provider, integrate them as a core part of our delivery model to afford optimized solutions for our customers? We believe that service providers will have to look at broader alliances with product vendors, OEMs, and other service providers (competitors) to give the "one company" experience to the customer in all future deals. Obviously, there needs to be a way to create simplified pricing around these opportunities where customers are shielded from multiple billing codes and invoices.

Underuse of the alliance ecosystem is a major focus for Nimma, from both the sell side and the buy side. After managing alliances and ventures for more than 10 years, while alliance-driven models are maturing, the center of gravity remains on the sell side as a go-to-market channel.

Nimma believes that in the current economic market there is a great opportunity on the buy side to request service suppliers to fully formulate turnkey offerings requiring demonstration of core competency alignment with the anchor supplier and its ecosystem. This would work not only for capability but across the dimensions of seamless offshore or onshore-based financial pricing, deal-centric and measurable operational improvements, with a shared goal of enabling the client to achieve industry competitive advantage (or meaningful improvement). True then, there is the game-changing matter that ecosystems designed for turnkey delivery are being disrupted by client-mandated cooperation. This in turn is forcing an alliance multi-lateralism that clients should benefit from noticeably, but that service providers are in various stages of adjustment to. Risk versus prosperity is the continuum traded off. Note that although this is a buyer's market (stating the obvious), the buyer's choices with this consideration in mind will result in a shift in the services-based competitive landscape. From an outcomes mind-set, it is challenging the notion that service-to-service alliances are a zero-sum game. Incorporating game theory will show it's not.

Alliances come in many forms. For large deals, the old-fashioned alliance model of selling services on alliance product revenues is not a winning formula. We are more interested in discussing the specific type of alliances prescribed here.

Joint ventures (JVs) are basically strategic tie-ups between two companies. They can be created by one company taking an equity stake in the other or by forming an independent company into which both parties invest resources. The goal is to feed off one another's strengths.

EDS has been extremely successful in India using the JV model. Satyam has been part of quite a few JVs. At the time of writing this book,

Satyam was involved in JV negotiations with a major telecom provider in the Middle East. Satyam and this customer have realized that instead of working simply in a traditional customer-service provider relationship, a true JV could benefit both companies much more. Satyam would bring its world-class information technology (IT) process and infrastructure and the customer would bring region-specific telecom domain expertise. The goal is to create a dedicated company for serving similar-profile customers across most Middle Eastern countries. Both Satyam and the customer would have joint ownership in the deal.

JVs can continue for an indefinite time and even become a separate brand. They may also operate on specific timelines. JVs using this model are sometimes called build-operate-transfer (BOT) models. This model is constructed on the premise that the service provider builds a delivery center for a specific period of time. We suggest at least three to five years as the lock-in period. At the end of this term, the customer takes ownership of the delivery center. The goal is simple: basically, the customer receives major assistance in creating its own captive unit, which should reap long-term benefits.

This model has actually helped niche service providers aspire to win bigger deals. We had an opportunity to meet Mirantis' managing partner, Sergey Shneyerson. Sergey, a Kellogg MBA, who developed a model where he can help Silicon Valley high-tech customers outsource their core research work to Russia. Mirantis' unique selling proposition is that it can enable U.S. companies to use high-end Russian engineering talent in a completely captive model. Mirantis builds the offshore center in Russia, hires the employees, and trains them to do the work. The work is typically managed by the client. Sometimes, they take a build-operate-own-transfer (BOOT) approach whereby they own the offshore property, run it as a separate entity, and eventually turn it over to the customer. Mirantis enjoys a handsome payday at the time of company transition.[2]

A number of Big Deals have happened recently that use this BOOT model. Barclays used Intelenet to build a mega business-process outsourcing (BPO) operation in India. Some of these deals have a different creative flavor. For example, Aviva Global Services (the sourcing wing of Aviva UK), owned and operated a captive offshore unit specializing in insurance and back office operations located in India before turning around and selling that operation to another BPO player called WNS for US$228 million.

But a strategic, alliance-driven model sometimes benefits a service provider a lot more than it does a customer. The story in Box 7.2

Box 7.2: How a Strategic Alliance Created a Multibillion-Dollar Business

In 1994, an IT services company was created as an in-house unit of Dun & Bradstreet. This company was a joint venture between Satyam and D&B. Satyam initially owned 24 percent and D&B owned the remaining 76 percent. By the end of 1996, the company became a unit of the Cognizant Corporation, after D&B was split into three parts.

By 1998, Cognizant had itself split into independent companies. The original JV, now called Cognizant Technology Solutions, became a division of IMS Health. IMS Health later divested all its Cognizant shares through a tax-free split-off. Today, Cognizant is listed on NASDAQ and has more than US$2 billion in revenue.

---

demonstrates how a multibillion-dollar service provider was created because of a strategic alliance.

Figure 7.1 illustrates a case study of a BOT model.

Being Innovative Financiers: When Service Providers Become Bankers

Today, no one can deny the uncertainty of the global economic market. Stock exchange indexes have taken an unprecedented nosedive, leaving well-known companies broke or facing a precarious future. Who would have thought that the stock of financial giants such as AIG, Citi, and Wachovia (now part of Wells Fargo) could be bought so low? Who would have thought that the booming economies of the tiger and the elephant, China and India, along with Brazil and Russia, would have been stopped in their tracks, or at least slowed down?

Surprisingly, this market turmoil has also opened up a tremendous opportunity for technology service providers to reinvent deal structures. Now, we actually have a situation where the service providers are sitting on a lot of cash and the customers are nearly flat broke. But for the customers to have any chance of ever regaining their market

Build-Operate-Transfer (BOT) in a Large Financial Institution

Service provider's responsibility
Enterprise backbone: disaster recovery, network connectivity
Enterprise infrastructure: servers, storage, desktop, call center, and network
  operations center
Enterprise applications: operating system messaging, database, core banking
  solutions
Branch solutions: desktop and related hardware and software
Enterprise security: network, application, and end user

Infrastructure solution	Product	Product or tool vendor	Service provider's unique value proposition
Data center hosting	Not applicable	Sify	- Scalability
Server and storage	IBM × series	IBM	
Branch desktop hardware	Ventura 200 v	CMS	- Availability
Telebanking	Aspect	Aspect	
Helpdesk application	CoDesk	IBM	- Manageability
Backup and recovery	Tivoli	IBM	
Email	Domino	IBM	

Customer's objectives		
Create end-to-end IT infrastructure		
Ramp up from 0 to 300 branches in 3 years		
Managed services for 10 years		

Figure 7.1 BOT Case Study

strength, they have to impose themselves with technology and process orientation. Efficiency in their operations will not be a choice, but a vital survival tool for the future. For many, it will be a time to perform some major core-business innovations.

So it's good news for us as service providers because we can help customers recreate themselves; there is really more business opportunity for us. But for service providers to take advantage of this situation and help our clients, we must find a way to get paid for deals. The advanced-pricing models can be great, but what can a service provider do if the customer lacks money? To be successful in the future, service providers need to see themselves as a one-stop shop with management consultancy, technology service delivery, and banking capability rolled into one.

In the next several sections, you will hear about some exotic instruments, such as financial structuring and structural solutions, that can be used in deal making. There is no denying that hearing about exotic instruments brings sheer terror and agony to the lay-person today. Who can blame people for questioning the merits of these instruments after recently witnessing a massive global financial debacle? Extremely smart bankers using all sorts of deal sophistication were able to successfully run their institutions into bankruptcy.

We believe that the problem was not in the instruments themselves but how they have been used. Greed, combined with an extreme attitude of high risk taking, resulted in bad deal making. Proper risk mitigation and thorough governance can make these instruments work. Because the global sourcing industry is a late entrant in this game of advanced deal structuring, we believe this industry will benefit from the lessons learned by the financial industry.

Here are some financial strategies that service providers can borrow from banks and financial institutions on how to be the lender of funds while also the provider of services.

Strive to Get Paid Early

Before we go into the details of how these advanced deals could be structured, let's understand a few basics about the time value of money. Suppose, as a deal maker, you have just signed up for a very large deal. Your estimated annual profit is US$30 million. Would you be willing to accept yearly revenue that contains US$30 million profit at the begin-ning of the year, for all three years? Or would you be interested in receiving all the money at the end of the third year? How about if we throw in a clause saying that if you wait to get paid until the end of year three, you get an added US$10 million bonus? Will the added US$10 million change your mind?

Well, if you received this payment in the yearly schedule prescribed earlier (US$30 million paid at the beginning of every year for three years), your total revenue gain, with 15 percent compound interest, would be US$119.8 million, which is about US$9.8 million more than the US$110 million (including US$10 million bonus) you would have received otherwise. In short, always strive to get paid as early as possible unless the end amount is much more than the added revenue gain from compound interest. It is not uncommon to find people questioning this logic. If you are including 15 percent annual com-pound interest on the earned amount, it implies that you are taking on an element of risk with the investment (why else will someone give 15 percent, when guaranteed CD rates are much lower?). Thus, mathematically speaking, if you factor in that risk element, you recognize that the expected value of the investment is lower than what you would expect by just looking at the compound interest from 15 percent. But most likely it will still be better than the US$10 million bonus received otherwise.

In the U.S., besides the interest rate earned you also need to keep in mind tax incentives and disincentives. For example, if you do not take US$30 million in profits every year but wait for three years to get paid, it is likely that you will pick up the "phantom" income in your taxable income and pay tax on it even though you haven't received the funds. So, if you get paid late by your customer, it is actually of no benefit whatsoever, from an earned interest standpoint as well as a tax standpoint.

But today, you are dealing with a sick economy (at least at the time of writing this book). Your customer does not have the money to pay you. It is up to you how you structure the financing to reach a win-win scenario. So far in all the chapters, we have talked about everything that we lived through. Either we did it ourselves or were part of teams where other members did exactly what we prescribed. But this section is speculative in nature. We strongly believe that service providers will do a lot more creative financing in the near future. Our ideas given here come from discussions we had with three finance and tax experts: Fazal Syed, a derivatives expert from a major U.S. commercial bank; Jeff Noland, investment banker and deal maker; and Sukh Saluja, who has extensive experience in international structuring services. We have taken ideas from these experts and aligned them with global sourcing principles. The next section is a refined list of what we believe will work in the global sourcing space, provided deal makers take help from banking, finance, and structuring experts to pull the deals.

Be Ultrasensitive in Analyzing Risks

Traditional IT services companies engage in risk analysis to ensure that customers will pay their fees for services. These service providers also do a risk analysis to ensure that project risks can be managed. But our experience says that service providers do both types of analysis while wearing an operational hat. Why not? They are actually operations-driven companies. But now, the time has come to think of service providers as bankers. We recommend every service provider be ultra-sensitive in doing risk analysis in today's shaky global economy.

Service providers need to fight hard to insert some new clauses into contracts. For example, a service provider has a full right to demand some sort of guarantee, maybe in the form of personal guarantees from customer executives, to be sure of getting paid. Although some people may think that this idea of using personal guarantees in publicly traded companies is pushing the limits, we think that in today's turbulent economy it is perfectly feasible. Executives with vested interest in keeping their companies afloat may be willing to use collateral guarantees. The customer will be more sensitive to paying you if its office building is held as your collateral.

We want to drive home one point, though. Banks focus a lot on risk analysis and mitigation on the basis of the industry involved. If you are serious about assessing risk, you need to engage ex-bankers, who specialize in risk analysis, to do this type of credit underwriting for you. You may want to instruct the bankers to be extra cautious when running risk models, given the current market dynamics. You need to come up with risk-mitigation strategies for recouping your investment if your customer cannot pay you. Using clawback clauses and obtaining warrants and notes for missed payments can ensure that the customer pays. But once you are convinced the customer can pay, how do you structure the deal financially? Here is a sample of ideas.

We believe that we will witness the use of covenants in global sourcing deals, similar to how a senior loan is sometimes structured. That is, the customer will be required to do certain things (perhaps maintain interest coverage greater than 1.2 times) or not do other things (such as pledge assets to someone else, in the event collateral has been taken, or undertake large amounts of capital spending without first seeking permission from its "lender", that is, you). There could also be limitations on future dilution, such that the warrants or equity taken back by the "bank" cannot be heavily diluted by future issuances of such securities. Finally, the lender (you) could require cross-default provisions, in the event that the customer defaults on other indebtedness that would also trigger a default on its junior indebtedness.

Use Financial Structuring

This structure may work in a deal where you believe your customer is short of money now but will be in a better financial position in a year or two. In this deal structure, the service provider delivers service for the customer and does not get paid immediately. The service provider actually bakes in an appropriate interest rate for delayed payment from the customer, taking into account the customer's risk profile. You, as the service provider, can also add in the risk-mitigation instruments described earlier as further assurance. So you are not just the service provider here, but also the bank. You are making money on the services delivered as well as making money on the financing leg of the transaction. The risk-mitigation tactics will help you cover yourself against the downside if the customer fails to pay.

This model sounds great, but there is a catch. Most of these risk-mitigation instruments (which are more like penalties), such as warrants and notes, that you have plugged in to ensure customer payments are junior in terms of their loan seniority. These junior debts are sometimes unsecured compared to other debts your customer may have taken against a traditional bank or other lender. So if the customer goes bankrupt, by the time the senior lenders get through with the customer there may not be any money left for you. A variation of the model may work best if you can rope in a third party to act as an insurance firm. This third party could be a bank, another service provider, or a neutral financier with a lot of money who can undertake third-party risk. The service provider pays a flat fee annually or periodically to this third party for its service. The interest rate here, minus the insurance fees paid, allows delayed receipt of the money.

But the third party does not always have to work on a flat fee. Instead you can craft a deal by using a common financial instrument called a "swap."

Banks have been using different forms of swaps to make money for years. In our example, the third party, who is the insurer, will actually get the money from the customer monthly or quarterly instead of you collecting it from the customer. The third party does the risk underwriting and understands that it will get the cash on time. The third party may even assist you in negotiating the interest rate that will be charged to the customer. You can strike a deal with the third party, who will pay you a fixed interest rate such as LIBOR + 150. (LIBOR, the short form of London Interbank Offered Rate, can in essence be viewed as a preferred rate that financial borrowers get, although technically it is not a preferred rate. LIBOR is a rate that banks use to lend money to other banks, so it represents an interest-free rate plus a premium.)

So as a provider you are guaranteed a fixed rate. The third party will make its money in the difference between the interest received from the customer and the rate it is paying you—which is LIBOR + 150 basis points in this case. It makes money on the spread. Now, the third party may also lose money if the interest rate charged becomes less than LIBOR + 150. This is where it will get tricky, with all sorts of term-sheet conditions to ensure that the third parties will get paid their fair share. Alternatively, the third party may find it feasible to pass on this risk to yet another party by entering into an additional swap agreement, on slightly more favorable terms. This approach of total return swap is an interesting concept because the third party gets the pointed end of the stick. You, as a service provider, are assured a base rate plus a specified margin. It is an interesting thought and can be incorporated, although swaps at the start are a zero-sum game. Syed (the derivatives expert) finds this model more attractive for third parties because they can make more money on the spread here.

The word *swaps* can cause much concern because the infamous "credit default swaps" have roiled the market recently. Overleveraging along with the failure of regulation within several financial institutions caused this massive havoc. Banks in the developed world peddled naked (no underlying collateral) credit derivatives, leading to massive margin calls. These positions eventually went against them, which perpetrated counterparty risk as the AIGs of the world went under. Incidentally, India is still nascent in its fixed income (bond) market, but if a deep market is developed with regulated trading of these instruments with conservative leverage, it can create an additional risk transfer mechanism and avoid the destruction from risk as witnessed.

In essence, swaps are a fancy word for insurance. By using a swap one is insuring oneself against the counterparty. There are several ways to use such instruments. First, by paying an up-front premium to the insurer/bank, one can mitigate the risk of failure of payment on the receivables or cash flows. One can also choose to have ongoing settlements where one pays a predetermined amount monthly or quarterly for the duration of the transaction in lieu of being made whole if the customer walks away. The benefit of having added insurance allows deals to culminate because worst-case scenarios can be taken into account at the onset of the deal. Also, having insurance on the cash flows aids the credit evaluation process of the counterparty because banks will be cushioned against the failure of receivables. Hence a deal that may in the past have required full equity financing can be transacted via debt leading to higher ROE (return on equity) numbers, thus enhancing profitability figures. It allows banks/insurance to make additional money on the spreads, and as the pool gets larger it helps them pool resources and manage their assets and liabilities. If done right, this model can be a win-win for multiple parties: service provider (client), customer, third party or parties, and the bank.

The key to success here is simplicity and prudence. If either the client or the bank starts using these instruments to speculate without adequate collateral, this will lead to disaster (as we have seen). One can draw a parallel to driving a car; if used judiciously and under proper guidance there is great benefit, but at the hands of a drunken person there can be a grim outcome.

Another way to look at financial structuring is to understand how the financing arm of IBM works. IBM is a true end-to-end technology solution provider. But it also has a division called IBM Global Financing, which offers simple, customizable leasing and financing for total IT solutions, including hardware, software, and services.[3] In simple words, IBM Global Financing can work as a bank in helping IBM customers pay for the services used from other divisions. Noland (the investment banker) asks, What is stopping a company like Infosys, Wipro, or TCS, or any of its peers, from becoming a sourcing-focused financial institution? The reality is that many large deals are still won by tier-two players. These deals could be simple volume-based staff augmentation deals where CSC, IBM, and HP rates may not be competitive enough to win. What is stopping any of these service providers from working with the tier-two leaders in these deals and becoming the third-party insurer? We do not know if BU leaders will be adventurous in going down this route, but it is definitely something to ponder.

Use Structural Solutions

The economic consequences of any financial arrangement are directly affected by how a transaction is structured. Generally, "structural," as used here, means legal structuring (both corporate law and tax), efficient-capital structuring (debt and equity considerations), and use of exotic instruments (hybrids and the like). Traditionally, banks have been the beneficiaries of such structural enhancements, given the requisite level of financial sophistication. Although we have used structural deals for global sourcing, we have not seen a majority of companies using such structural solutions consistently to optimize deals. It is no surprise that traditional non-banking companies tend to shy away from sophisticated structural enhancements. Who would blame them, after what happened to companies such as Enron that got caught abusing structural enhancements to cheat stakeholders? Saluja (the structuring services expert) warns that structural solutions require constant monitoring and a dedicated team to assess the impact that changing legislation (as with that for taxation) has on implemented solutions. As such, one has to be extra diligent and hire the best advisors before going down this route of implementing structural solutions. But the rewards could be immense if done right.

Even so, service providers can try a trusted old strategy of using other people's money (OPM) in becoming lenders to customers. The conventional wisdom is that debt is cheaper than equity. For example, if a service provider's project cost is US$500 million, it expects a 20 percent ROI and funds the entire project cost with equity; in a best-case scenario it would get a US$100 million return. With a tax rate of 30 percent, the service provider will really make US$70 million on that US$100 million receipt. Now, in reality this equates to a 14 percent return after tax. But if the service provider finances a portion of the project cost, either from a larger service provider or from a bank, the service provider is basically using OPM to achieve the same objective. In this example, if the service provider borrows US$300 million and uses US$200 million of its own money to pay for the project, it will have the necessary US$500 million. Assuming the service provider's cost of borrowing is 10 percent, the service provider then pays the lender US$30 million in interest expense. Still, assuming a 20 percent ROI here as well, the service provider earns US$100 million dollars before taxes and interest expense. The return, after interest expense, is US$70 million and taxes on this are US$21 million. As such, the service provider ends up with a net profit of US$49 million. So here the service provider really invests US$200 million of its own money and gets back US$49 million in net profit, which is a 24.5 percent posttax return. It sure looks better than a 14 percent return to us. Clearly the percentage overall return, as the amount the service provider invested, decreases (and the return is actually infinite if US$0 of one's own money is invested). So why stop at investing US$200 million? Why not borrow the whole thing? It is primarily a matter of being overleveraged. We all know the fate of overleveraged homeowners, financial institutions, and other businesses during the recent subprime crisis.

The example here gives a basic illustration of the benefits of an optimal capital structure. Another example of structural enhancements is extracting value from the financial attributes of a customer. For example, a customer may have carry-forward net operating losses for tax purposes, which may be expiring. Under the right facts and circumstances, a legal structure could be devised such that the service provider and the customer employ a structure that affords cost savings or financial enhancement to both.

But it's not just about using customer tax losses as a shelter. What if, as a service provider, you do not take cash back from the customer as payment for your service and instead you opt for other instruments? Let's demonstrate this with a simple example.

As a service provider, you are supposed to receive US$30 million in cash from your customer. For the sake of this example, let's assume that all of the US$30 million is profit. Let's also assume that instead of taking cash you structure the deal such that you get US$20 million in preferred stock and US$10 million as dividends on preferred stock. Further, for the sake of simplicity, let us assume that the alternative arrangement does not incrementally increase the customer's costs. Saluja tells us that U.S. corporate entities receiving dividends from other U.S. corporate entities can get a 70 percent tax break on the dividends received under certain conditions. So, assuming that the deal can be structured as described, although you receive US$30 million cash you are simply taxed on US$23 million because US$7 million of the US$10 million dividends will get a tax break. In simple terms, if this service provider is supposed to pay 30 percent tax on US$30 million profit, ordinarily it would amount to US$9 million but in the structured alternative the service provider pays US$6.9 million. This results in a saving of approximately US$2.1 million. Now, think of the rewards if the service provider can structure this deal format earlier and share the benefits with the customer during the deal-pursuit process. Will this help you win the deal? Structuring experts (accountants, lawyers, and financial consultants) from different jurisdictions can help structure deals like this for specific regions of the world.

A point to note in this example is that there is a significant difference in the service provider's credit exposure to the customer in the structured case. To be specific, in the base case the service provider has a trade creditor's exposure, while it has a preferred equity investor's exposure in the structured case. As such, the provider needs to be comfortable with and able to manage this new exposure. Also, if you get stocks as opposed to plain cash, you have less liquidity and become subject to stock price volatility. As a business, you need to judge how important liquidity is as far as this transaction is concerned.

But this is just one example. The benefits of structural solutions go much further. Most of the named global service providers are registered in many countries of the world. There are certain countries that give significant tax breaks to companies. For example, say your fully owned subsidiary in one particular country does business with a customer in another country. If your subsidiary is in a country where you pay little tax or almost none, you and your customer can both gain from it. Your customer can show the revenue paid to you as costs and deduct it from taxable income. You, on the other hand, do not have to pay the taxes completely or fully on the received amount because of the tax breaks. As a result, you can actually factor in the tax advantage and charge the customer a lower rate. Again, this is a simplified example to illustrate how structuring can provide business enhancements. Real solutions would require extensive research and an understanding of the laws of the relevant jurisdictions. We are noting this because we believe these avenues should be explored further and evaluated to see whether there are opportunities available to service providers.

Conclusion

In this chapter, we have explored a few creative business and financial strategies to optimize your deal structure. The goal is not to convince you to use any particular strategy over another. The goal is to get you thinking about how, in today's economy, deal structures will change. It will be beneficial for all of us deal makers to think about deal structures beyond the services industry model. We believe that many of you will customize deals on the basis of many new innovative models in the years to come.

Notes

1. "BPO Clients Seek Upfront Payments." *IndiaTimes*, Dec. 15, 2008. http://infotech.indiatimes.com/Outsourcing/BPO_clients_seek_upfront_payments/articleshow/3838741.cms.
2. "Assessing Outsourcing's Build-Operate-Transfer Model." *Outsourcing Insider*, Sept. 16, 2008. http://www.blog.infinit-o.com/2008/09/assessing-outsourcing%e2%80%99s-build-operate-transfer-model/.
3. For further information, see http://www-935.ibm.com/services/us/financing/index.html.

CHAPTER 8

Doing Contracts Right

Creating the Foundation of a Successful Marriage

Contract terms and conditions are a necessary evil. By the time the contract negotiation stage comes around, both the customer and the seller are exhausted after having been put through the wringer for so long. Both parties want to close the deal and move on. Sellers are especially motivated to get the contract over with because they can smell the money from their commissions or variable bonus payout. The reality is that in a traditional, back-end, staff augmentation, global sourcing model, there was always minimal importance given to this stage of the pursuit cycle. The customers and the service providers were trained to put their stamp in the right boxes, initial next to the Xs, and sign along the dotted lines for the deal to get done. Even when a dispute arose, it was never severe enough to challenge the validity of the contract itself.

But large multi-year deals (Big Deals), often with fixed pricing, are a different beast altogether. As the size of the deal grows, the contract tends to get more and more innovative and complex. It is easy for the customer or seller to interpret contract clauses differently if they are not explicitly clarified. The story in Box 8.1 will make you consider why businesses need to be ultra-sensitive during this phase of business.

The story in the box is a perfect and common example of mixed interpretations of legal clauses. But before we can think about how to fix such a conundrum, we need to understand large contracts better.

What exactly is a contract? To us, a contract simply means two things: (1) a legal deliverable and (2) a business deliverable. A contract should also specify broader deliverables such as outcome, risk, and changes; basically, the incentives and disincentives.

A renowned outsourcing lawyer and global sourcing expert from a prominent UK law firm defines a contract by the term "meeting of the minds." Now, this term has a different legal dynamic to it. It actually means intent. So if we analyze the story in Box 8.1, was the customer

---

Box 8.1: The Mega Effects of Missed Communication

Recently, Anirban was having a conversation with a partner from an eminent New York law firm. The topic of discussion was mixed interpretations of global sourcing contracts. This partner (who we will call Rodney for the purpose of this story to spare any guilty parties) was representing the buyers of a mega global sourcing deal. His customer, a large U.S. corporation, was in the midst of a potential lawsuit with a prominent services provider. The customer was not happy with the services and wanted to get rid of the service provider. The service provider was willing to let go of the contract, so long as the customer guaranteed a fee of US$200 million per year to the service provider for the next four years. The customer laughed, looked at the contract, and decided that the service provider was nutty at best and greedy at worst.

Well, maybe the service provider was not as nutty as they originally thought. When the case was initially evaluated by lawyers from both sides, it seemed as though the contract did not say that the customer had to pay almost the entire total contract value if the work was taken away from the service provider. However, the contract was worded in such a way that the master service agreement was to be read along with all the local service agreements, exhibits, and so on and so forth, possibly to marginally decipher the intent of the contract. If somebody did read all 15 or so of these documents, the service provider might get the idea that it could qualify for a US$200 million-per-year handout under the reduced resource credit (RRC) clause. All in all, there was a big disparity in how this contract could be interpreted from the buyer and the provider perspectives.

---

willing to pay a US$200 million-a-year penalty if the contract was scrapped? It seems as though the service provider thought so. This scenario is not unique. You will often see reports coming from major analyst organizations and research groups saying that more than half of global sourcing deals fail. On closer observation, you will find that these deals do not really fail in the typical sense, where the service provider could not deliver the promised artifacts. In reality, it has more to do with customers not getting some of the perceived benefits they thought they would get. It is a case of missed connection, where the intent was not clear during the meeting of minds. Without knowing the details of the case mentioned in Box 8.1, it is hard to tell whether this scenario of an apparent missed connection was created by design or not.

Our extensive experience in doing Big Deals has taught us a few basic lessons. Too often, the business leaders from both the service provider and the customer side tend to believe that most of the items in a contract are legal terms. Who can blame them for thinking so when all they are hearing is legal verbiage such as *force majeure*, indemnity, and RRC? But if you think deeply, most of these are basically business terms; that is, these clauses will have a direct business impact (it does not have to be a legal impact). For example, *force majeure* dictates what happens in an unforeseen event. As a business leader, you need to ensure that the other party is not using *force majeure* as a vehicle for gaining unfair advantage. We came across a situation where the customer demanded to pay less because the price of gas went up, hurting its core business. Now, although a northbound gas price hurts all of us, let's get real: is it an act of nature causing massive destruction? However, one could argue that *force majeure* is a matter of interpretation. What's *majeure* for you may be *mineure* for me. To make a long story short, we believe that business leaders on both the provider and customer sides need to have an explicit understanding of all terms and conditions and make a judgment call with regard to what matters to them.

Our goal is not to make you a legal expert by the end of this chapter. As a matter of fact, we are unqualified to do so. But we want to cover some of the basic elements of Big Deal contracts that you should be aware of as a business leader. The actual process of negotiating the contracts is a chapter by itself and is covered in Chapter Nine.

The Basics About Contracting (What Every Deal Maker Should Know)

We believe every deal maker should know about a couple of things related to contracts: the master service agreement (MSA) and the local service agreement (LSA).

Master Service Agreement (MSA): What's It All About?

An MSA is a contractual document that highlights all the essential contract terms between the customer and the service provider. The

MSA is much broader than the traditional staff augmentation contracts associated with purchase orders or purchase agreements. MSAs define a more expansive business relationship between the service provider and customer. Typically, senior business unit leaders, deal makers from the Strategic Deals Group or its counterpart, and lawyers go over the MSA to assess what is acceptable and what is not. Fundamentally, there are two circumstances under which a Big Deal happens between a customer and a service provider. In scenario one, the customer and the service provider are already in business with one another and a basic business understanding between the two parties is well documented. In scenario two, the customer and the service provider may have limited or no existing business transactions between them. Under the first scenario, an MSA is already in place that dictates the basic understanding and the rules of business between the two parties. Under the second scenario, an MSA needs to be put in place. Although there are many ways an MSA can be written, experienced deal makers suggest that every MSA should contain detailed contract terms but leave the commercial details and the scope to be documented separately under projects or towers. This enables the pricing and scope to be addressed at the tower or service level.

One basic tenet is that the contract language should *not* be cut and pasted from your proposal! Proposals are a sales tool, used to persuade the reader of your capabilities. They purposefully paint as rosy a picture as possible without falsification. We believe every MSA contract should have all these points addressed as a bare minimum:

- *Specific terms and conditions (T&Cs) of the relationship* Although service providers and customers spend significant time clarifying the intent, they often fail to impart specific meaning to common understanding. For example, what does the sentence "The service provider will strive to increase the time to market for the customer" mean? This comes directly from an RFP response that we worked on in the past. Is *strive* definitive here? We think not. It is critical to be specific on what you are actually trying to say, leaving minimal ambiguity. We suggest business leaders write this section in simple English but keep it detailed enough to remove all ambiguity. An alternative to that phrase would be to say "The service provider will take concrete, measurable steps to increase the time to market for the customer. Definition of these specific steps will be created according to the recommendation of the provider and the customer participated governance council."

- *Transfer and transition clause* "Transfer and transition" is a clause that never used to make it into MSAs before. Today, it is mandatory. As a service provider, you need to be extremely clear on how your customer is planning on transferring such items as knowledge, responsibilities, and cost allocations. Do you really know how your taxes will be affected or how you can amortize the infrastructure and equipment that you will inherit? How about transferring people? Are you considering all the ramifications, such as salary and retirement clauses? Transition is an important topic by itself and is addressed separately in Chapter Eleven.

- *Broader governance* MSAs should contain a detailed governance plan on how project and program managers will manage their work. But the overall escalation procedure, executive briefing, and key performance indicators (KPIs) need to be identified here to remove ambiguity. This section should definitely address how the overall reins can be kept on all projects to assess quality. There must be complete clarity of roles and responsibilities. If the project is a true staff augmentation under a larger overall scope of work, the risk in customer operations does not pass to the service provider or seller who is just supplying "bodies" while the work is directed by the customer.

- *Termination clause* Relationships terminate in two main ways: normally or abnormally. Normal termination is when the work is done and the contract ends; typically this is referred to as expiration. However, there are also abnormal situations, such as termination for cause, for convenience, or for "jeopardy." The cause- and convenience-related termination clauses are quite self-explanatory. The contract can be terminated because either party behaved inappropriately, or failed to meet the performance standards agreed to in the contract, or simply wanted to walk out. Termination for jeopardy relates to sudden regulatory changes or legislative prohibition; for example, what if the Indian government suddenly says that India Inc. cannot work for companies based in Israel? Termination clauses should detail penalties, work transitions, and employee transfers from service provider to customer.

- *Intellectual property (IP)* Previously, IP concerns were related only to data security. Today, however, service providers are working hard to make IP for customers but getting paid only for services delivered. Service providers are now asking for a stake in the IP game. Later in the chapter, we detail some thoughts on how IP needs to be handled for large deals.

- *Legal and regulatory provisions* There are some legitimate legal and regulatory provisions of which a service provider should be aware. When doing business with a customer, we suggest you look out for industry-specific regulation (for example, Office of the Comptroller of the Currency regulation for banks and offshoring in the United States), country-specific regulation (such as the USA Patriot Act and privacy laws), and employment-specific regulation (the Acquired Rights Directive regarding employment in Europe) among other things. Invest in good lawyers to dissect such laws.
- *Provision to handle exhibits* All Big Deals have plenty of exhibits. Exhibits are like additional chapters, sometimes also called appendixes. These exhibits are details on certain clauses. For example, the MSA might have a section on termination. This section might refer to a certain exhibit, which will detail several clauses regarding termination. The MSA needs to be read with the exhibit. It is essential that the MSA be written for clear instruction on how exhibits are to be read. Going back to the story in Box 8.1, we can say that the contract was not structured in this way. There should not be a disparity between how the service providers view the contract and how the customers look at it.
- *Dispute resolution* Many Big Deals end up in dispute. Service providers should encourage customers not to run to court every chance they get. We believe a thorough mediation structure must be put into the contract. This mediation structure should detail all the possible ways of resolving disputes before going to court. Later in this chapter, we highlight some of the ways in which you should encourage your customers to handle disputes.

Local Service Agreement (LSA) or Statement of Work (SOW): The Land of Price and Work Promises

An LSA contains the commercial details and the scope of the service provided for a unit of work. For example, a Big Deal between CSC and a major telecom provider could span multiple countries, technologies, and domains. An MSA can detail the overall business relationship, but there may be several areas within the business relationship that require specific attention. The LSA deals with specific business areas such as departments (for example, payroll), technology (application development and management), and towers (infrastructure management services). Although senior leaders make the call about the content of an

MSA, it is essential to get the delivery managers, project and program managers, and architects involved in LSA contract drafting. We believe that all LSA contract terms should have the points addressed here as a bare minimum:

- *Roles and responsibilities* This is a key area of the contract specifying exactly what you are required to do as a service provider. You can project the specific roles that you are going to furnish here. This is also an opportunity for you to have the customer put a stake in the ground. For example, you can link this section with the one on transition where your customer needs to supply a certain percentage of subject matter experts (SMEs) during the transition.
- *Scope of work* This section is the work deliverable that you are responsible for. Be clear about what you sign up for. When specific projects happen within a Big Deal, customers often expect more than what is under contract. This is called gold plating. It is important that you have clear definition of the exact work and not engage in gold plating.
- *Commercials* Commercials (also called pricing) are probably the most looked-at item in the contract. This shows how much the services will cost and addresses how the customer will pay. Commercial structures are described in detail in Chapters Six and Seven.
- *Scope-specific transition* Although general transition requirements are defined in the MSA, project- or tower-specific scope should be defined here. This is the chance for business leaders to have their specifics regarding the delivery of such items as systems and servers addressed in detail.
- *Performance metrics and status* Managing KPIs is a key factor for the service provider. Most projects are perceived as failed projects because service providers cannot align their results with the KPIs the customer is looking for. Service providers need to spend a lot of time aligning themselves with the customer on what KPIs they will be measured against.
- *Project and program management* This is a subset of overall governance. The key project deliverables and the project and program management structure need to be defined here. Project and program management should map to the overall governance strategy.
- *Warranties, rewards, and penalties* We think most Big Deals should have an element of warranties, rewards, and penalties. As a service provider, you should include some warranties on some clearly acceptable criteria. If you beat them, you should be rewarded. If

you do not meet them, your customers will expect to slap you with a penalty. Be hard on this contract term by making sure that the rewards at least equal the penalties, if not outweigh them.

- *Change management* When we interviewed several CIOs and buy-side business leaders for this book, most of them mentioned change and risk management as their greatest concerns in the global sourcing environment. The service provider should clearly define and spell out their change management and contingency-planning procedures. One of the main ways CIOs are measured is how long the technology systems and applications can operate without a major breakage causing business disruption. CIOs understand that disruptions are part of the business and systems will break. What they are typically keen to know is how well the service providers are positioned to fix breakage by applying change management and contingency-planning procedures to get the systems and applications up and running quickly.

Avoiding the TPA Trap: Some Red Flags for the Service Provider

Almost every service provider will concede that TPAs have successfully guided many contracts in favor of the buyers, on the basis of their knowledge of what certain service providers have already agreed to in other deals. This leverage has created some thorny legal risks for service providers who are fairly successful in pushing the risk bar back closer to even play. Here are a few risks to review carefully, so as not to underestimate them if assumed risk is not negotiated.

- *The sweep clause* This clause, without carefully negotiated wording, has the legal connotation of "sweeping" into the service provider's SOW any activity previously performed by customer personnel who are now working for the service provider (whether related to IT or anything remotely technology-based). The clause relates to the scope of work assumed by the service provider. It states that no matter what duties were performed by the workforce previously, the service provider is now obligated to perform the same duties in the future (see Box 8.2). Make this requirement as specific as possible. For example, if the scope of work under contract is applications only, then try to limit the scope to "include only work performed in relation to IT applications".

Box 8.2: When a TPA Misused the Sweep Clause

After nine months of detailed negotiations and hours of legal and business wrangling, a contract for more than US$1 billion was about to be signed by the two parties. The existing service provider's 435 client associates were transitioned to the new service provider, whose due diligence determined that they were fully used only about 75 percent of the time. The new service provider's strategy was to leverage these resources across multiple clients, thereby saving the customer money and justifying the deal. However, it turned out that nearly all of the bench time or unused IT work time was spent doing volunteer work for local charities. The new service provider did not consider these tasks to be within scope, and charitable volunteer work was not an explicit (or even implicit) part of the MSA, LSA, or the SOW. Therefore it could be "discounted" to achieve savings for the client. However, the sweep clause, if left as recommended by the TPA to the customer, would require the service provider to do *all* the activities previously performed by customer personnel, regardless of its relevance to the MSA draft. Caveat provider!

- *Service-level credit pool and stake allocations* TPAs are pioneers in taking up concepts used in other industries, such as construction, where performance standards are critical in ensuring that buyers receive the quality of services for which they contracted. TPAs skillfully apply these concepts to the global sourcing business. For buyers to turn over the "keys to the store" in a managed services engagement, the service provider must agree to a service-level credit pool, typically, from 10 to 30 percent of the monthly charges. This amount is what the service provider is willing to forfeit to the customer for missing the service level (a performance guarantee). Be careful when signing contracts with regard to the service-level credit pool.
- *Benchmark pricing* In long-term agreements, customers often need to ensure that the prices they lock in stay competitive over time. Benchmarking provisions allow price comparison over time. However, if not negotiated, these clauses may require you to automatically drop down to a lower price if the benchmark study

---

Box 8.3: Seller (Service Provider) Beware: Two Horrifying Tales

Tale One: When Benchmarking Stinks

We know of a deal where a service provider entered into an agreement and this clause was left essentially as proposed by the buyer. A benchmarker determined that, in the second year, the service provider's pricing was 25 percent higher than the determined benchmark. The provision in this clause required the service provider to immediately reduce all pricing to the lower levels, which consequently made this deal unprofitable. In this particular case, the parties chose to terminate the agreement, but not without the service provider taking a major financial hit.

Tale Two: Limitation-of-Liability Trap

In another mega deal we know, service provider executives flagged a line that said *"prime contractor is responsible for any and all third-party obligations under the agreement, including the buyer's right to lost profits."* This line was part of the limitation-of-liability clause. It was determined that if left uncontested the service provider's exposure through this clause was essentially unlimited. In short, although the limitation for items subject to this provision was two years' revenue, this exclusion could expose the service provider to potential insolvency over the failure of a third party's performance.

In conclusion, there are a fair amount of *provider beware* items in these transactions.

---

warrants it (see Box 8.3). This provision also allows the customer to terminate the agreement for cause even if just one pricing element is determined too high. We recommend that you position the clause to include these conditions:

1. The benchmark must be normalized to include similar circumstances such as volumes, performance standards, and other considerations often traded off in overall pricing.

2. Allow benchmarking in subsets of the overall agreement. If the benchmark is off in one part, then the remedy is valid only against that part.
3. Make dispute resolution available in non-court settings (that is to say, contract escalation within the governance model of the relationship).

- *Limitation of liability* Here, there are numerous factors to consider, such as the "limit" itself as well as exclusions from the limit. If you are not careful you could risk your entire firm on one contract's liabilities. Typical limits are one to two years of contract revenue on multi-year deals. Offering the limit to be the overall contract value or higher should be avoided at all costs unless the size of the agreement is small enough to warrant some discussion.

All About IP: Why Not Knowing This Can Take You to the Cleaners

We have decided to focus on intellectual property as an entire subsection because IP-related litigations are on the rise. It is also difficult to draw a clear line between what is acceptable and what is not when it comes to IP.

According to Wikipedia, "Intellectual property (IP) is a legal field that refers to creations of the mind such as musical, literary, and artistic works; inventions; and symbols, names, images, and designs used in commerce, including copyrights, trademarks, patents, and related rights. Under intellectual property law, the holder of one of these abstract properties has certain exclusive rights to the creative work, commercial symbol, or invention by which it is covered."[1]

So what does the legalese from this extract really mean? Simply put, IP is the conceptual product of the company, its bread and butter. It is no surprise that customers get up in arms if they feel a supplier has violated the terms and conditions relating to IP. There are many statutes that encourage, incentivize, and promote creation of new artifacts that boost social and economic growth. The watchdog for IP protection is called the World Intellectual Property Organization. WIPO is focused on two main areas of IP infringement in the global sourcing model: ownership of IP, and accidental or willful transferring of business knowledge. Protectionist charters are put in place by regulatory agencies worldwide to deter others from stealing IP. This is to ensure that individuals or companies creating artifacts feel motivated to share the creation and enjoy the monetary benefits associated with the creation for a given period. The tenure of IP protection is finite, after which the knowledge and its free use are usually transferred to the public domain.

There are many types of IP, classified into broader sections.[2] However, for the purpose of this book and audience, we focus on the major types that large global sourcing deal makers need to be aware of:

Copyrights are designed to protect tangible creations such as artwork, music, books, articles, drawing, painting, sculpture, and photography. These items are typically protected for the duration of the copyright owner's lifetime and an additional number of years.

Trademarks are unique and distinguished signs, marks, and logos that exclusively identify a commercial good or service that a particular enterprise or individual produces. The trademark owner gets the exclusive privilege to use the trademark to sell, market, and license the good or service delivered. Various countries work as governance and jurisdiction bodies and offer a stipulated period of protection for the trademark.

Patents are rights granted for a product or a process that is a new way of doing things. Effectively, they protect a new solution for a problem. The inventor (an individual or a company) is the exclusive and legitimate owner of the right for the new solution for a specified period of time; 20 years, in most cases, from the disclosure of an invention. The right protects the legitimate owner against being excluded from monetary benefits if somebody else uses the invention for commercial purposes. Typically, patent owners have the right to decide who can use the patent, whom to license it to, and whom to sell it to. Patents not only generate monetary benefits or protections against monetary fraud but also offer the author a chance to be recognized as a legitimate leader in that space. Eventually, patents expire and become available to all in the public domain.

IP Security Best Practice: Steps to Mitigate Potential Pain

There are all sorts of ramifications that can come up in an IP scenario between the service provider and the customer. A major lawsuit in a Texas court, between a renowned technology services provider and a European mobile-payment specialist, has attracted special attention because of the implications of IP for all technology services companies. The case is also interesting because it does not deal directly with ownership of a patent or stealing patented work. It actually represents contract-related litigation regarding the transfer of a patent in a complex global sourcing scenario. We believe that this lawsuit (in court in 2009) opens up new contractual frameworks between customers and technology service providers relating to innovation and complex service delivery. The story in Box 8.4 is a lesson on why deal makers (and customers) need to be hypersensitive in drafting contracts related to IP.

Box 8.4: The Muddy Waters of Patents: How a Major Lawsuit Could Have Been Avoided

The customer in question is a European mobile-payment specialist. In the mid-1990s, this customer wanted to create a capability whereby it could convert any phone to a prepaid phone. The model was that consumers using this phone would call a number where they would supply details of their personal prepaid account, give the associated personal identification number (PIN), and then be connected. The customer drafted a short, informal contract with the chosen technology service provider to develop the underlying software.

Toward the end of the 1990s, this customer applied for a patent for this product in the United States. The type of patent sought required establishing "unity of ownership" of the intellectual property rights and the associated invention, basically proving that the customer owns the IP. However, the product was created by the service provider. The contract between the service provider and the customer dealt primarily with service-level agreements, with brief mention of the ownership of inventions and IP-related clauses. The customer assumed that the service provider was going to turn over all the IP rights. The net result was that the customer ended up with the intellectual capital by paying a cash amount to the service provider in 1999. Once this was settled, it seemed that, at least for the time being, the saga was closed.

(continued)

Although so far it has proved troublesome to acquire the patent, this was only half the story. The agreement concluded in 1999 had a specific clause stipulating that this agreement went hand-in-hand with a prior 1998 agreement between the customer and a specific service-delivery unit of the service provider that was working on the customer product. Both the 1999 and the 1998 agreements had to be read together. The 1998 agreement had a specific clause dictating that the IP rights would be sent back to the service provider if the customer stopped paying for services.

The service provider, at this point, owned one-quarter of the customer through a debt-equity exchange. A few years later, the customer started complaining vigorously about the declining quality of work by the service provider. The service provider vehemently denied the allegations, blaming the customer for trying to get out of paying for services rendered. The service provider pushed for the IP rights to be reverted back to them, and the customer accused the service provider of IP infringement. The professional environment became too unhealthy to continue business as usual. Finally, with the help of capable mediators from both sides, the turmoil came to an end as a settlement agreement was reached between the two parties in a European court. This settlement overrode all previous agreements.

Several years have passed since, but it seemed that the gods were against these companies. The customer started a new lawsuit against two parties (not the service provider) for infringement of its IP in a U.S. court. The original service provider was called in to testify on behalf of the customer because it did the work as part of the agreement. However, this new court case brought the validity of the customer IP into focus. It was not so much who owned the IP as whether the IP that the customer claimed as its own did actually belong to the customer. Allegations of misconduct and fraud now entangled the customer and the service provider. As a result of this accusation of fraud, the customer was awarded a verdict that they did not quite agree with in the U.S. court's judgment.

Not too long ago, the customer sued the service provider again in a U.S. court, alleging fraud and consequent breach of contract. The case goes to trial in 2009.[3]

It is clear from the story in Box 8.4 that neither the service provider nor the supplier thought of a prenuptial agreement before they got into the marriage. Well, this marriage went bad. The lesson learned here is that it is vital for the service provider to clearly establish the contractual terms and conditions for IP before creating artifacts for the customer.

But drafting a contract for IP is not that simple. Customers and service providers do not completely understand how to play in the muddy waters of IP. We frequently run into the Nervous Nellie customer who simply wants to be super-safe. These customers want to nail down every IP-related provision early in the game, even before the technology solution has been put in place. This is almost impossible to do. Customers need to sit down with service providers to understand the impact of all the IP created, so that they can mutually decide who keeps what. If the IP is going to be a value differentiator for the customer, they need to control reuse of the IP. If the customer is certain of gaining monetarily because of the IP, the customer should insist on owning it. But if the IP is part of a process that has been sourced, a process the customer has no interest in harvesting, why not give it to the service provider as a negotiating tool? The service provider can negotiate for software, data, business and technology processes, trade secrets, inventions, and know-how, as well as other confidential information and works of ownership. Service providers need to be clear regarding clauses related to knowledge and expertise gained while working for the customer. It is unreasonable to assume that a service provider employee will not be enriched with process knowledge or subject knowledge once he or she has worked on it for a while. It is unacceptable for the service provider to agree on any term that frowns on knowledge transfer.

Our strong recommendation is that service providers work closely with lawyers who have experience in dealing with IP-related issues pertinent to global sourcing. NASSCOM (introduced in Chapter Three), a well-regarded organization for global sourcing providers, and IAOP (see Chapter Two), the international association for global sourcing professionals, may be able to help service providers find legal professionals in this field.

We are not 100 percent certain it is possible for the service provider and the customer in a technology-sourcing environment to create a contract that is IP-infringement-proof. Although seeking protection for software is an expensive endeavor, industry leaders who are experts in IP-related matters tell us that software patents, or technology components that use a lot of software, are prone to fraud. But this does not mean that deal makers and BU heads should sit and do nothing about protecting their interests. We offer three thoughts on how to protect yourself from IP-related hazards:

1. Thorough IP due diligence
2. Achieving IP protection
3. Creating legal protection of IP

Thorough IP Due Diligence

Developing technology in a globally sourced environment is a complex scenario. For a project to be successful, there needs to be a tremendous amount of data sharing between the customer and the service provider. Technology products also contain thousands of components, making it nearly impossible to conduct a full patent clearance on every product. What happens if, during the supply-chain mechanism of creating a customer component, a dispute arises over the IP of a small component that was used as a part of the whole product? It can derail the overall product initiative and even trigger an expensive lawsuit. We believe that IP due diligence involves a number of items:

- *Joint effort in IP prioritization* Often, your customers will not want your opinion on prioritizing IP. They will want to decide for themselves which IP they want to keep, which IP belongs to a third party such as a product service provider, and which IP the service provider can keep. It is critical for you to truly understand the scope of the work associated in creating the IP that the customer wants to keep. Of course, you want to understand the scope for all the work you are going to do for any customer, but special attention needs to be paid in this case because customers tend to sue more frequently when it comes to IP-related problems. This extra diligence will also help you determine if the work associated with the IP needs to be classified as high-, medium-, or low-risk so that proper strategies can be built around it to mitigate the risk. Also, you need to know whether the IP you are dealing with is of any real value to your organization. You can bet that the customer will use it as a negotiating lever. Always beware of third-party IPs; our experience has shown that many unethical customers try to demolish service providers by exercising IP-violation threats if they even sniff a possible transgression.
- *Breach prep* If you are running a large, multi-country, multi-year deal with a customer for whom you are creating a lot of IP, the

chances are that your team will unknowingly breach some IP-related contract. Be clear on all dispute-related procedures, including mediation and legal recourse. Also, we recommend that you maintain an almost-real-time register that documents the type of IP, the ownership, the expiration date, the contract terms around it, and the association of IP with service provider–implemented work.

• *Offer acceptable assurance* We are great believers in being transparent. Show your customer how you plan to stop IP infringement, as with misappropriation, misuse, theft, loss, and sabotage. You must demonstrate a thorough IP protection and data security process document, as well as physical and virtual IP security (such as locks on doors as well as password, fingerprint, or even retina scan access to data). It does not hurt to show that you follow some standardized compliance initiative, such as Sarbanes-Oxley (SOX), even if it is not mandatory. This gives customers peace of mind believing that any IP infringement can potentially be tracked back to origin (even if this is not always true).

Achieving IP Protection

IP may be the customer's most valuable asset. As a service provider, it is our inherent duty to help customer organizations deal effectively with all types of IP-related issues, including providing electronic and physical protection. Here are some of our thoughts on this topic:

• *Need-to-know access* As a business leader, you must assure your customers that only a select few have access to their core IP. These people must have a distinct need to use that IP to create a service for the customer.

• *Physical security* As a service provider, you may be unfairly cast as representing an organization that does not care about IP security. Many people will be more than happy to take a swipe at you by giving examples such as the case of British customers' confidential data flying around the streets of Bangalore. You need to have high-end physical security: electronic access control through biometric means (retina scan or fingerprint) or 24/7 video monitoring. Also, we have seen some successful business-process outsourcing (BPO) and information-technology outsourcing (ITO) providers use almost paramilitary security in frisking employees to detect removable media such as disk drives.

- *Electronic security* Service providers are also responsible for ensuring that a data breach does not happen because of such malfunctions as system lapses and system downtime. Under no circumstances should there be access to such items as source code and patented designs for anybody outside the need-to-know personnel using them. Test data should never contain real information. You must also have a prevention plan if you intend to use freeware or open-source code to deliver products for your customer.

Creating Legal Protection of IP

Although you have a defined contract with your customer in which it is clearly stated what the legal recourses are, we strongly recommend that you specifically highlight the legal protection for customer IP during negotiation. Some things you may want to consider:

- *Legal structures defined* As a service provider, you need to articulate to your customers how, in which court, and under which circumstances, IP disputes will be resolved. You can rest assured that a customer in Midland, Texas, does not want to tangle with a judge debating in Vietnamese in Ho Chi Minh City. We need to draft contracts so that IP disputes can be resolved in an arena where both the service provider and the customer feel comfortable.
- *Government influence* In many countries, governments take a leading role in curbing IP infringement. After a few unpleasant experiences in India, the government of India took stern action by imprisoning people responsible for IP theft. Such news, demonstrated with evidence, will help the customer be more at ease.

Resolving Disputes in Big Deals: How Not to Go to Court

Disputes happen. Just ask any married couple. The analogy of commercial contracting and married couples is often used to illustrate dispute management. It is also imperative that best effort should be made by all concerned parties to resolve disputes without going to court. Court proceedings will be costly and painful, and typically take a long time. For corporate strategies, our best advice is to resolve disputes before they land in court. Courts bring massive legal fees, delayed justice, and prolonged headaches. Alternative dispute resolution (ADR) offers an effective and cheap way of resolving disputes without going to court.

Alternative Dispute Resolution

ADR is a common approach that is getting a lot of traction these days for resolving disputes related to large-scale global sourcing. Historically, India has always championed a form of ADR for resolving all disputes. Villages have local bodies made up of village elders called *Panchayats*. These bodies mediate disputes between villagers. Today, corporate use of ADR is being recognized by courts as well. Many courts actually help the warring parties by furnishing them with ADR tools.

ADRs are becoming popular because they offer a number of benefits to customers in contrast to traditional courts:

- *Cost* ADR costs a fraction of what it would cost if the parties decided to go to court to resolve a dispute.
- *Time to closure* It may take 10 years to get a judgment on a case. ADRs tend to resolve disputes in months.
- *Collaboration* Both the supplier and the service provider have more of a say on what type of ADR to use, which panelists will be the judges or mediators, the duration of the process, and sometimes even the result. The informal process also encourages better dialogue between the service provider and the customer.
- *Fairness* The third parties assigned to resolve these disputes are experienced mediators who can do this work well and guarantee a better outcome.
- *Confidentiality* Because the dispute does not reach the courts, there is an almost non-existent chance of a breach of confidentiality.[4]

In addition to the common forms of ADR (dispute-resolving negotiation, arbitration, and mediation), there is also online dispute resolution (ODR).

Negotiation

In the dispute-resolving negotiation form of ADR, the service provider and the customer engage in lengthy discussion, trying to resolve the conflict. There is no third party to mediate. But sometimes this form of dispute resolution is not enough.

Mediation

If your relationship with your customer is so bad that good-faith negotiation won't work, try mediation. Parties often use an independent third party, such as a legislator or a community leader, to mediate a dispute. The parties decide the rules of engagement and terms of agreement. The third party does not make the call on the dispute but acts more as a checking and balancing point. The third party ensures that the warring parties have thought through all the implications.

Box 8.5: When Mediations Fail: The Nano Story

Some of you may be familiar with a major dispute that has grabbed national headlines in India for the past two years. The dispute is between Tata Motors and a political party in West Bengal. Tata Motors embarked on a massive project to build the cheapest car in the world, called the Nano. The Nano project enjoyed the limelight in such respected publications as the *Wall Street Journal* and *Business Week*. The proposed project was great for Tata, but it was an absolute game changer for the state of West Bengal. The state needed not just investment but also publicity asserting that it was an investor-friendly state. West Bengal is a major Indian state that has lagged behind in economic development, compared to its peers, for decades.

But an opposing political party, the Trinamool Congress, created major distractions that lasted for two years, making it difficult to establish the project in the city of Singur, the proposed location. There were strikes, demonstrations, bombings, and attacks on Tata employees; name a particular tactic, and it was used here. The main dispute was regarding land rights. The West Bengal government allotted land to Tata that it acquired from local farmers. However, the Trinamool Congress did not support the land transfer for this project. Although Tata built initial infrastructure to do the work out of Singur, eventually it decided to halt work indefinitely, citing security hazards.

In 2008, the West Bengal government finally realized that they could not convince the opposing party to let Tata do the work. The West Bengal governor (a non-political post in India) was

(continued)

---

summoned to intervene as the mediator between the West Bengal government and the Trinamool Congress. This governor was well respected by most people in the state. He tried to bring all the parties to the table and work out a win-win scenario. After lengthy mediation, it seemed that the parties had agreed to common ground. In early fall 2008, the media was flooded with news that agreement had been reached and work was shortly to resume at Singur.

But soon after the agreement, it seemed that the parties went back to their own demands. The communist government of West Bengal blamed the Trinamool Congress for changing the terms after agreeing to the ideas. The Trinamool Congress blamed the government, using the same accusation. Nothing changed for the better.

Finally, in October 2008, Ratan Tata, head of the Tata family, made the decision to move his Nano project to another Indian state, Gujarat. With that decision, the dreams of millions of Bengalis were shattered.

In this particular example, the mediation did not work and Tata moved shop. It shows that mediators cannot be enforcers.

Arbitration

Arbitration is another approach that could have been used in the example of Box 8.5, when mediation failed. Many service providers prefer to work with customers using this method, where a third party is engaged who actually makes the judgment. The hearings are private and much more informal than court hearings. But we seriously doubt that it would have worked in this example either. If a major political party is against a movement, a lawsuit may be the only way out. However, with lawsuits of this magnitude in India it has traditionally taken an eternity to deliver a verdict, so this option may not have been feasible to begin with.

Online Dispute Resolution

Online dispute resolution (ODR) is another innovative dispute-resolution technique. A major Indian outsourcer has used this technique in the past for recovering domain names from a cybersquatter.

Conclusion

Negotiating with your customer on contract terms can be quite rough and complex. Never undertake these endeavors without appropriate legal involvement. As stated elsewhere in this book, a self-representing service provider in legal or other professional matters, without adequate legal and business area subject matter expert assisting, has a fool for a client. It is imperative to write contracts in clear and understandable language. We also recommend that you put key details in the contract so that there is little or no ambiguity on what is expected versus what is delivered. This is, however, easier said than done. Is it better to sign a less-than-perfect deal? Or is it better to keep on negotiating in the hope of perfection at the risk of the deal falling through? At what point do you say "Good enough"? This is a call to be taken by the leaders of individual service providers. We recommend that if there is a good business relationship and trust with the customer, then it is OK to be a little ambiguous in the contract and not prolong the negotiation. But for brand new customers, or for customers that are ready to go to court at the drop of a dime, it is better to be as clear as possible in doing contracts. No matter how deliberate both parties are in constructing a great contract, a deal is not a deal until both parties sign. Never underestimate the competition, as millions of dollars bring about "creative" last-minute solutions.

It is also mandatory, in today's technology-enabled world, to truly understand and bargain for your stake in the high-value IP game. And finally, think of litigation as the last option. Collaboratively working with your customer and using ADR strategies to resolve disputes will help you continue a relationship with your customer that is much longer than the period that the latest large deal you sold will last. Happy contracting!

Notes

1. See Wikipedia entry for "Intellectual property" at http://en.wikipedia.org/wiki/Intellectual_property.
2. Satyam Computer Services, "Legale Communique," Sept. 2008, *1*(1), 2–4.
3. Satyam Computer Services (2008), pp. 2–4.
4. Chandrashekaran, S. "Satyam evam Upaid: Who paid?" *SPICY IP*, Jan. 18, 2008. http://spicyipindia.blogspot.com/2008/01/satyam-evam-upaid-who-paid.html.

CHAPTER 9

Closing Big Deals

It's Commercial Negotiation, Baby!

Dictionary.com describes negotiation as a "mutual discussion and arrangement of the terms of a transaction or agreement."[1] The process for closing any deal begins with the subtle negotiation skills of two parties: the customer and the seller (service provider). Simplistically speaking, in the context of global sourcing a successful negotiation leads to a signed contract between the service provider and the customer. Negotiation is (often mistakenly) viewed as sales evangelism. We believe sales evangelism to be the process whereby sales professionals communicate with customers to move the sale forward. This sales evangelism process can be as simple as a dialogue with a customer by the water cooler, or it can be a formal sales meeting or series of meetings. Most negotiation books cover sales evangelism techniques in detail.

As you have seen so far, this book is focused on the multiple dynamics of closing big global sourcing deals (typically US$50 million TCV). These deal closures are similar in nature to securing funding for larger projects or closing significant mergers or acquisitions. These types of deal pursuits can last for several months, or even a few years. Skilled sales professionals are adept in moving a Big Deal through the sales evangelism stage into the commercial negotiation (also colloquially called contract negotiation) stage. Commercial negotiation is a fairly detailed formal negotiation session between the customer and the service provider that lasts for several days, sometimes even many weeks or a few months. Pricing (Chapter Six), advanced deal structuring (Chapter Seven), and legal and business terms (Chapter Eight) along with transition (Chapter Eleven) and governance (Chapter Twelve) clauses are advocated throughout this book. These clauses are discussed in detail during the negotiation session(s) between the customer and the service provider. Sometimes customers and service providers are aided by external lawyers or consultants to help them through the commercial negotiation discussions. The end result is a successful signoff (or not, if both parties cannot reach a common ground) on the deal.

This chapter focuses on aspects of doing commercial negotiation with your customer. Hetzel once saw a Ferrari with a license plate that simply read FUNDED 1. When you've finished reading this chapter, you'll have a much deeper appreciation for what that plate really meant—as he did when he saw it.

Ten years ago, outsourcing meant sending non-core work to an external outfit. The customer mentality resembled "lift and shift." Today, customers outsource core businesses not just to save significant money but to leverage operational efficiencies and gain domain competencies so as to increase long-term profitability. These Big Deals, at a minimum, consist of customers transferring entire BUs, people, processes, and intellectual capital to external providers. More often than not, these deals are essentially mergers or divestitures camouflaged as traditional out-sourcing. Big Deal negotiators should be extremely comfortable with discussing how to break up percentages of onsite and offshore resources and the hourly billing rates of developers, and also with discussing asset valuations, historical earning valuation, discounted cash flow, relative valuation, multi-country labor and commercial laws, and tax loop-holes—things that are essential in merging two businesses or taking away part ownership from another. Additionally, one must be culturally aware so as to pacify egos, clarify agendas, and most important not fall prey to conflict stemming from lack of cross-cultural communication. Negotiating successfully in today's multi-cultural world is a crucial topic and is addressed later in this chapter.

The challenge in closing large multi-year deals successfully is to understand the complex dynamics involved. Sizing up the players involved in large deal negotiations is critical to a successful outcome. Amateur negotiators and ill-prepared business teams can break a deal, or even worse win a deal that either loses a lot of money or brings unreasonable risk. But in today's global marketplace, the worst fate for Big Deal negotiations may be the loss of time and money, spent over many months, on a deal that just will not close.

Things grow complicated when the customer hires a paid consultant to lead the negotiations on their behalf. Service providers sitting on the other side of the table now also have to access what motivates the consultant. To make matters worse, the customer plans on parallel negotiations with the competition. Do we, as service providers, know how the competitor negotiates? What are the price points? How flexible are they in the terms and condition (T&C) negotiation? Is the incumbent working with the customer? What started out as a two-party deal now has multiple players, with varying interests. If you've ever negotiated a two-party deal through a third party "agent or consultant," you will most certainly agree on two simple facts:

1. Their deals almost always close.
2. They are more complex and detailed in their structure—generally a better deal for all parties.

Although this chapter will not make you a large deal closing expert, it will give you a taste of what it takes to negotiate large outsourcing deals involving savvy negotiators from multiple cultures.

Assembling the "Dream Team" of Large Deal Negotiators

Negotiating Big Deals is an exact skill requiring professionals to do it well. Many global sourcing service providers engage in these deals with a team consisting of non-negotiation professionals from the BUs. These people were once good programmers who graduated into good delivery managers or directors. Or sometimes this group of negotiators consists of good sales people who are experts at getting their way in sales evangelism situations. Although this group understands technology management well and has successfully negotiated millions of dollars of small outsourcing deals, which required moving resources around on a time and materials (T&M) model over the years, they do not have much experience in negotiating large merger or divestiture outsourcing deals. This lack of understanding about the complete ramifications of these deals tends to make these rookie negotiators extra cautious and extremely risk-averse, which in turn often leads to a common outcome: walking away from the negotiation table.

A Big Deal negotiation team should, at a minimum, consist of four people: a deal director (also called the capture executive), a financial or pricing strategist, a commercial or legal strategist, and a solution specialist. It is advisable to get this group of people to stay together and participate through the entire course of the commercial negotiation. This core group takes support from the sales team. Many a time, we have seen lawyers pop in and out of these meetings, wanting to participate only during the legal discussion part. This is not good

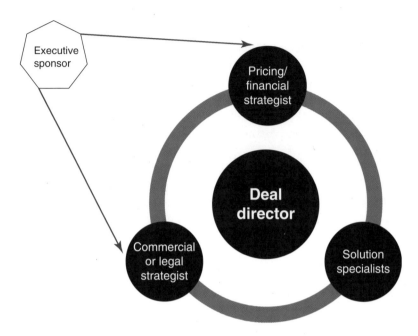

Figure 9.1 Dream Team of Big Deal Negotiators

because it breaks the group synergy. Besides, a big part of the decision making goes on behind the scenes during the negotiation preparation, where everybody brings a unique perspective. We talk about negotiation preparation and atmosphere in a later section of the chapter. There is obviously cost associated with keeping this team together for the entire course of the negotiating cycle. Typically, the bill is paid by an executive sponsor from the participating vertical business unit. Figure 9.1 shows the dream negotiation team composition.

Deal Director

A deal director (capture executive) is responsible for directing the entire pursuit. He or she engages from the early stages of a deal, sometimes in the pre-RFI or RFP stage to get the deal going. Deal directors work with the sales leaders in various account teams to identify or create Big Deals. If the deal has any TPA or external consultant involvement, then the deal directors also work with the TPA relationship manager to engage with these external paid consultants. Deal directors are the main architects in guiding the entire pursuit by leading from the rear (Chapter Five). Because the deal directors know the deal dynamics in and out, they are an essential element in monitoring, validating, and participating in the commercial negotiation.

In large service provider organizations, it is almost impossible to satisfy every BU in winning a deal. Let's look at the hypothetical example of a large company, a BU in telecom eager to win an SAP implementation deal in Japan, under any circumstances. Assuming this company has limited penetration in the Japanese market, this win may help get a large market share there. However, it is quite possible that the SAP practice is really focused on growing a European presence in the current year. They are budgeted to spend significant money in Europe and do not really want to divert to Japan for a one-off deal. However, the greater good of the company dictates that SAP practice should focus on Japan in this case. Here the BU representative plays a big role in internally negotiating so that everyone is on the same page, and consequently so that the negotiation team can act as a joint force in front of the customer. A deal director performs the delicate role of constantly balancing the needs of corporate and all participatory technology and business facing units engaged in the deal.

Financial Strategist

A financial strategist (also interchangeably called a pricing strategist) is responsible for shaping and negotiating the economics of large and strategic deals so that the service providers can compete effectively for new opportunities and achieve their financial objectives. Typically, financial strategists understand pricing, M&A, complex contract structures requiring the purchase of client assets, rebadging of client employees, data center acquisitions, third-party subcontracts, large procurements, leasing arrangements, and telecom agreements. Financial strategists take the lead in risk management and pricing guidance in large deal negotiation. During negotiation, these experts lead all financial aspects of deal creation (Chapters Six and Seven).

Commercial Strategist

An ideal commercial or legal strategist should have expertise in labor and commercial law for the countries that the deal is associated with.

This person deciphers legalese (legal language in contracts), helps craft legal terms and conditions pertinent to the deal, and finally leads the negotiation to ensure that the service provider is not stuck with unwarranted liabilities. Additionally, the legal strategist, in conjunction with the financial strategist, can guide the service provider and the customer on use of tax loopholes and tax shelters (also called structural solutions) to maximize benefits without asking for a lower price. Practical, real-life methods for using advanced deal structuring of this type were shown in Chapter Seven. Commercial strategists take the deep dive on all issues related to contracts, as defined in Chapter Eight.

Solution Specialist

This technology superhuman participates in the entire negotiation process to ensure that the service provider is not committing to any technology delivery promise that it is not feasible to deliver. For example, this person dictates and validates the skill levels of delivery resources that are committed to the customer. Also, this person ensures that the work estimates described in the MSA are broad enough to cover technology innovation, advancement and change in terms of application, and the delivery technique of technology solutions.

Besides this core group, if any Big Deal requires people transfer (rebadging) then it is imperative to have an HR presence in the negotiation room. Similarly, if a service provider is looking at buying part of the customer business, then M&A teams, corporate strategy, and corporate finance should also be involved in the negotiation. For more than average Big Deals or deals that have other strategic importance, BU heads or deal group heads also participate actively in the deal.

Inside the Deal: Deal Room Expertise

So, what happens in a negotiation room? Is it like the old movies where everybody is in a suit and tie, sitting across the mahogany table from one another and discussing terms and conditions while smoking a cigar? Or is it similar to the board room in the TV show "The Apprentice," where a Donald Trump-like person exudes charisma while dictating terms? Although all these situations can be true, there is no hard-and-fast rule on the negotiation room setup. Typically, three or four people from both customer and provider sides sit down and hash through the items on the negotiating agenda. The customer generally drives the atmosphere. If they require suit and tie, they tell you that in advance. Typically, you should know from your team's prior interaction whether the customer organization is formal or more casual; prepare accordingly.

The process of negotiation can get quite intense, though, and it all begins a week or so beforehand. The provider's negotiating team should meet in a war room (a designated conference room or hotel room) where all preparation for this upcoming negotiation will take place. The team expects the customer to send a filled-in contractual document (an MSA, LSA, or something similar) to the provider with their position on all terms that are up for negotiation. Good deal directors should not wait for the term sheet to come in and start the process. They should begin role playing way in advance and assess all possible positions the customer can take on every issue of the term sheet. We suggest that you itemize all the topics under consideration into four categories: *extremely important, important, workable,* and *trivial.* For all the topics under consideration, start listing your positions with a preference. You should have a preferred position, a secondary position, a tertiary position, and an unacceptable position on every issue. The best way to decide these positions is to understand the impact. Let's take an example of a hiring clause (Figure 9.2). The clause says that the provider cannot hire any customer employee.

In the figure, the service provider cannot accept the position defined in the last row. The rest can be accepted, possibly in the order shown. Now, imagine that this item is extremely important, and the provider has to hire customer employees to succeed. You are sure that the customer will object and won't budge on positions one, two, or three. Amateur negotiators might break down and walk away here. Experienced negotiators will try all avenues in understanding why the customer is so rigid on this item (maybe they have been burned by a provider before). The provider should then start negotiating on the penalty aspect of the clause breakup. Does it still matter as much, if the clause stays as is but the penalty for failure to comply is reduced drastically?

This is where negotiation becomes an art and not a science. You can chart all the positions, but it is the convincing skills of the negotiators and the ability to map issues (issue one: hiring; issue two: penalty) such as the ones described here that can be the difference between making and breaking a negotiation.

Provider Preference	Preferred Position of Customer	Benefits and Drawbacks
First	Service provider can hire any customer employees anytime, anywhere.	Service provider can gain knowledge and retain it in-house.
Second	Service provider can hire specific customer employees only after securing explicit permission from customer.	Service provider can gain knowledge as long as customer allows it; scope is limited.
Third	Service provider will not knowingly hire any customer employees.	Position is OK if the business is good. Drawback is that service provider will have to work longer to understand skill sets.
Unacceptable	Service provider will not hire any customer employees under any circumstances.	This term is too restrictive. How can you stop an employee of this customer in another country from being hired by the service provider?

Figure 9.2 Negotiating Position Analysis

Let's assume for a moment that the term sheet has come with the customer's terms. The deal team, with all their practice, quickly fills in their position and sends the term sheet back. This new provider position is shown in, say, Microsoft Word Track Change mode, so the provider and the customer can track differences in positions. A day or two later, both parties convene face-to-face and start debating the points one at a time.

Before walking into the actual negotiation with the customer, it is mandatory to assign a lead negotiator. This person does not have to be the deal director and as lead negotiator will have the right to stop negotiations at any point. He or she can also break ties and make critical calls on behalf of the provider. Generally, the lead negotiator handles the extremely important issues, and maybe the important ones. Sometimes, the easier ones are pawned off on the others who can be "good guys" and give in as per the master plan. We recommend the commercial strategist take the lead while discussing legal terms (maybe with the help of a lawyer) and the pricing strategist lead pricing negotiation even if they fall under the headings extremely important or important.

It is common for deal teams to use signs or gestures to direct people to slow down or change course, change position on the fly, or even suddenly go rigid and play games if necessary. Although we do not promote guile in negotiation, you may often see mind games and dirty tactics employed by a customer. We have dedicated a section entirely to how to tackle negotiation tricks. But more common is a problem that can be defined by the words "lost in translation." Today cross-cultural negotiation takes on a life of its own and is a vital topic for Big Deal negotiators.

Multi-cultural Negotiation Best Practices

Being properly understood is obviously critical to doing business abroad. However, avoiding offending cultural sensibilities is an equally essential element of global negotiation. The more professionals understand particular business cultures and customs, the more valuable they are to their organization. However, those who miss the individual norms of people doing business with people will still struggle and scratch their head over the money they continue to spend on deals that never close.

The story in Box 9.1 describes how teams matter in closing deals.

Box 9.1: When Communication Fails: Cultural Outlook Matters Always

Hetzel was once involved in a JV negotiation with another large global service provider. The customer was trying to get into a contract, where Hetzel's team, the service provider, would invest to build and operate a dedicated offshore operation for them. The agreement would allow both companies to jointly pursue outsourcing deals worth several billion dollars. At the end of a specified period, the service provider would transfer the offshore delivery operation to the customer and walk away with fixed revenue and some residual revenue to be paid over a number of years.

The negotiations with the other company were going really well until it came to deciding on the terms of the exit plan. (A valuable lesson: always get agreement on your exit strategy *before* closing the deal.) The customer, familiar with this type of negotiation, suggested that at the end of the term they take ownership of the offshore business at asset value. However,

(continued)

Hetzel's team balked and insisted on giving up the business in whole or in part only at market value—typically, a multiple of annual revenue.

There is a big difference in outlook here. Hetzel's team wanted to leverage the upside of economic growth and get market premium at the end of tenure, whereas the customer wanted to limit their liabilities and upward financial premium and pay asset value only. Asset value would most likely be much less than market value. Both parties were right in their outlook in terms of representing their stakeholders' interests, and as such they demonstrated differing though acceptable positions.

Maybe, culturally speaking, the Indian businessmen on Hetzel's team were more protective of their investment. It is also possible that the Western businessmen represented by the customer saw this protective gesture as pure risk averseness. Good commercial negotiators, proficient in cross-cultural communication, are experts in managing a situation to reduce massive disconnects between parties and within parties. Cultural, or just savvy, negotiators on both sides in this case demonstrated that not all negotiations conclude in a contract, and that is not always bad news.

Numerous courses, designed to teach professionals how to negotiate successfully across cultural barriers, are available in today's marketplace, and many are quite effective. These courses offer helpful pointers that enable businesspeople to appreciate the customs of the people with whom they would like to work. However, most have a key limitation: they make little mention of the multi-cultural businessperson. Courses that offer communication techniques based on geographic or ethnocentric generalizations, for example, may be accurate. However, their applicability is diminished significantly in today's flat world.

Consider the case of a particular CEO of a fast-growing, multi-million-dollar, privately held, alternative investment firm. The CEO, Indian by origin, was born in Algeria and grew up in that country. He moved to Canada as a teenager, and then to the U.S. for college. Throughout his career, this gentleman has traveled extensively and spends significant time hopping around all over the world. As such, he has absorbed the intricacies and complexities of many cultures. He has also developed the ability to think and behave multi-culturally. Psychologists call this skill "frame switching."[2] An increasing number of multi-cultural customers have developed the ability to switch frames because of an upbringing that exposed them to various cultures. It is often true that they were born in one country, lived in several others, travel the globe frequently, and perhaps married a person of an ethnicity different from their own. Along the way, they have subconsciously absorbed a second, third, or fourth culture, without supplanting those they already understand. People with multi-cultural minds—people who can switch frames, like this business-savvy CEO—are often valuable business assets. They are intelligent, are multilingual, and understand local and global business environments. As businesses become more global, frame switchers are more apparent. This can be troublesome for less sophisticated businesspeople. For instance, how does one negotiate with a multi-cultural professional like this gentleman in a Big Deal negotiation? It would be a mistake to assume that he would "behave like" an Indian, Algerian, Canadian, or American. In fact, making an assumption of any kind about such a complex personality would be risky.

In the next section we explore four general best practices that could be applied by the negotiations team during cross-cultural business negotiations.[3] All are designed to remove emotion and preconceived opinions from consideration, ensuring a rational, businesslike approach that reduces the influence of factors such as geography, ethnicity, and educational background.

Take a Non-positional Bargaining Approach

This technique is easier said than done. People who do commercial negotiation are bound to encounter hostile behavior from time to time. Typically, the other party vigorously asserts its theories as to why a proposal is absolutely unacceptable. Inexperienced negotiators tend to sell their position more aggressively at this point. They expect to convince their adversary with crisp logic.

This hardliner approach usually leads to one of two results, neither of which is positive. The other party will continue to defend his or her position, probably escalating hostilities. Or if cornered by logic, he or she may feel belittled. Winning the argument might bolster a negotiator's ego, but it will not help form a long-term partnership. Successful cross-cultural negotiation requires sensitivity and tact. Only then can a mutually beneficial solution be worked out. Here are several key steps to a non-positional negotiation approach[4]:

- *Acknowledge the customer's concern* The workplace can be a sensitive environment. Understanding the customer's pain is a way to start off on the right foot. It also validates feelings.
- *Do not endorse the customer's concern* There is a big difference between acknowledging and endorsing. Endorsing an opposing position deflates an argument before it begins. Do not agree to an opposing position, but disagree tactfully.
- *Highlight the situation* Negotiations can be difficult and require meetings neither side wants to endure. Address the fact honestly. Mention that both sides were dealt a tough hand, but the problems can still be resolved cooperatively. Being honest and having empathy leads to more concessions than anything else does.
- *Focus on customer issues (discovery and resolution)* Focus on the customer's issues and figure out how to alleviate that pain. Remember, this is why the customer is talking to you in the first place.
- *Focus on customer (personal) gain* Many senior customer executives are ambitious and individualistic. Learn—in a tactful way—what these executives are measured against, and then craft your solution to those parameters. Everyone enjoys this part of the conversation.
- *Seek genuine help in championing your effort* There is no shame in asking the other side for help. Try to understand what the other side is attempting to achieve, and ask them to help you develop a mutually satisfactory solution.

Articulate Fact-Based Information

Staying on point while communicating—verbally or in writing—is an invaluable trait. Leverage documented case studies, proof of fiscal health, industry and analyst views about the organization, and lists of awards and accolades that the organization has earned in relevant competencies or lines of businesses. Eagerness to win business can lead to information overload; inexperienced negotiators tend to furnish far more information than necessary. Sending a simple, clear note about agenda items one would like to discuss is also helpful. Northwestern University professor Jeanne Brett, a specialist in cross-cultural negotiations, recommends this approach and says that responses to proposals should be crisp and to the point, without overglorification of achievements. The ability to simplify complexity is powerful. Recently, a high-caliber negotiation team Anirban was part of bid for a multi-million-dollar deal with a high-tech customer based in Silicon Valley. Negotiations stalled on several items in the MSA. Rather than eliminate the issues of contention and cave in, the team placed them in a spreadsheet. The columns illustrated proposals and counterproposals, as well as possible compromises. The next day, with the facts and figures clearly visible and easily digestible, the problems were re-solved. Emotion and adrenaline had been removed from the equation.

Play the No-Guessing Game

This is a critical, but often overlooked, negotiation rule. Experienced negotiating professionals tend to analyze customer responses, actions, and trends to make business decisions. However, this analysis is based on guesswork and is often faulty. Big Deals mean dealing with influencers, lobbies within the customer organization, and special financiers such as private equities and hedge funds, all of whom have a vested interest in the customer. As such, it is critical to under-stand all agendas and express an accurate position.

Mahan Khalsa, a renowned sales negotiation expert and author of *Let's Get Real or Let's Not Play,* suggests that negotiators who sense ambiguity should step back and "see, hear, and feel" the problem, and then find a tactful way to address it.[5] This is a principal part of getting real during negotiation. Early on, determine if an issue is a yellow (traffic) light that can be resolved through compromise or a red light—a showstopper that cannot be resolved. Too often, red lights (matters that preclude mutual understanding) are hidden for as long as possible, so that negotiations keep moving forward. This can be a massive waste of time during negotiation. Work hard to address problems that can be resolved. But be prepared to walk away—to get real—if an issue arises that absolutely cannot be solved.

Practice Reference-Based Persuasion, Rather Than Status-Based Persuasion

In today's flat world, it's crucial to leverage reference-based persua-sion. Sometimes, especially in the middle of a deal, it can be wise to introduce new faces to negotiations. However, selecting the right team is paramount. Many inexperienced negotiators bring in executives early to add weight to their argument and help convince the other party to buy into their idea. There is a time and place to demonstrate executive support (especially in the later stages of negotiation cycles). However, early on it is more valuable to negotiate on the basis of merits and references. At this stage, it is more effective to introduce a practice head (a reference for a specific competency area) or an existing customer who can share relevant experiences. Proactive, reference-based discussions go a long way toward moving deals to the commercial negotiation stage.

Provider Beware

As much as we would like to tell you that the intention of all service providers and customers is to get to a win-win scenario, the reality is different. There are a whole bunch of customers out there who engage in active gamesmanship to promote their cause. Big Deals tend to bring these borderline unethical tactics to the forefront. Below are a few common ruses that we have run into while negotiating Big Deals.[6]

- *Be wary of quick wins* This is a common negotiation technique used by both customers and service providers. Accept right away several demands from the other party having low business impact. This shows a willingness to close the deal. However, if you see too much of this happening early in the negotiation cycle, prepare yourself for the storm. We bet that your customer will continue hitting you with difficult requests and expect you to accept them, as you have been doing.
- *False deadline* "If we cannot sign the agreement today, the deal is off." Be wary when your customer applies time pressure on the day of the meeting to get you to commit to an unfair deal. Time is a valuable pressure tactic. Tell your customer you are trying to create a true solution for them. It is important that you truly understand their issues first and do due diligence. It is unfair to you and your customer if you commit to something you do not feel comfortable about. If they do not want to listen and instead they force the time issue, it is your call whether you want to budge on their unilateral demands or walk. Personally, we feel you should not succumb to time pressure.
- *Wrongful summary* The other party summarizes the agreement but misrepresents certain sections in its favor. If you listen especially

carefully to the wrapping-up part of the negotiation, you will not fall into this trap. You should take notes and refer back to them if necessary to make sure that the summary accurately describes what you agreed on. This happens every now and then during contract negotiations.

- *False importance to an item* A great deal of importance is placed on an agenda item that your customer knows you simply cannot move on. They make you feel guilty, putting the pressure on and hoping that you will give them other concessions to make up for the one you could not give in on. One way to avoid this is to treat each issue independently and make separate decisions.

- *Shock effect* Regardless of how much value selling and convincing you have done, at the end of the deal when the time comes to discuss price many customers show some shock effect. "What! That much for SAP software support charges, are you kidding me?" It is easy to fall into the trap of desperately wanting to close the deal and offer unnecessary concessions such as free services, and lower onsite rates for resources. This will be a good time to remind your customer how they will truly benefit from using your offerings. Also, it is not rude to tell them that quality products have a fair price; after all, you get what you pay for.

- *Ongoing discount* Have you ever heard something on these lines? "We are so close to signing this contract, if only we can solve this last issue . . ." You oblige, and then out comes another issue, followed by one more, and then another. Soon, you are giving away much more than what you originally intended.

- *Prioritization* It is good practice to list all customer issues early in the sales cycle on the basis of priority. If new issues are added, put them on the list and reprioritize. When your customer asks about resolving this one last issue, get a firm commitment on closing the deal right after the issue is resolved. In this way, you might end up giving in to only the last demand and not the ones still to come.

- *Boss knows best* We have all spent countless hours discussing value propositions with customers, convincing them to buy from us, only to find out that they are not the true decision makers. They can only negotiate to receive discounts but do not have any rights to actually close the deal. In this case, we have basically negotiated with the wrong person. One way to avoid this is to ask early in the cycle how the decision to buy is being made on the customer side. Who makes the decision? Who influences the decision? Especially for high-end technical sales, a CIO may often have the final say on the procurement, but she is dependent on the wider business to make the call on the service provider. It is important to identify the players involved in the decision-making process and talk to them individually or collectively to resolve their issues.

- *Delays* March, June, September, and December are hot months for deals teams trying to sprint to the end of the quarter. Although progress has been made, your customer is deliberately delaying making a decision. Many manipulative customers feel they can count on the fact that you have spent a lot of time and money on the sales process and will not want to go back without closing. This will be a great way to snag a few concessions. It is wise to stay as emotionally detached as possible, rather than caving in and making unnecessary concessions to close these deals. Remember that your customer has also spent valuable time with you in the sales cycle. You both have an interest in the outcome. Don't rush to closing; you have mutual benefits tied to the deal.

- *Suddenly cold* Many customers like to play this mind game while trying to engage a service provider. They seem interested in the early stages of the negotiation process, and then all of a sudden they lose interest in the service provider. When the service provider pursues their interest again, the customer engages. But this time they try to dominate from a position of strength. They attempt to remind the service provider that they really do not need the service. This is a good time to tell your customers again why they should pay you what you think they should pay you. Craft your message on what's in it for them to engage your organization.

- *New player* You feel you are moving along well and suddenly you see a new person negotiating with you. He wants to start discussing every item from scratch and does not want to acknowledge previous agreements. If you cannot pursue him to honor prior understanding, start fresh again. It may be good to get another negotiator from your side as well, if you go back to square one, because you may get frustrated dealing over the same issues again.

As hard as it may sound, negotiators are better off remembering that the dirty tactics used by manipulative individuals are never really personal and it is all part of the game. If you are fair in your dealings and stay emotionally detached, you are more likely to negotiate your way to a win-win result.

Conclusion

Skillful negotiation is critical, and usually the only way deals move forward. Convincing a customer to consider service providers as allies is easier if a service provider delivers crisp, factual information; uses the right people to move a deal forward; and avoids ego battles with customers. Additionally, negotiators should ask questions to ensure that they understand a client's situation and its entire ecosystem—its customers, partners, suppliers, investors—as clearly as possible. Guesswork is not an option.

Negotiation is often viewed as dispute resolution. We tend to forget that we all negotiate every day to resolve disputes in our personal lives. We do it without even realizing that we are actually negotiating. One day, during the course of writing this chapter, Anirban saw his two-year-old twins vigorously fighting over a special toy, a music-playing snail. Soon mom arrived and by having a discussion with the children was able to stop their fighting. The toy was temporarily removed from sight and later brought back, after which both of the kids played with it peacefully (at least for the time being). Mothers everywhere negotiate with their kids to resolve disputes without ever acknowledging that they are skilled negotiators. The point here is that we should all go into a negotiation session with the attitude that negotiation is a natural thing and we can all do it. Just as Barack Obama said in his U.S. presidential acceptance speech, "Yes, we can."

Notes

1. See http://dictionary.reference.com/browse/negotiation.
2. Michael Morris, Chi-yue Chiu, Veronica Benet-Martinez, and Ying-yi Hong, "Multicultural Minds—A Dynamic Constructivist Approach to Culture and Cognition," *American Psychologist*, July 2000, 55(7), 709–720.
3. Anirban Dutta, "How to Negotiate with the Americans," *Rediff News*, May 24, 2006. http://in.rediff.com/money/2006/may/24anidut.htm; Dutta, "The Art of Front End Negotiation: Mastering the First Step in Winning Large Outsourcing Deals," *Sand Hill.com*, December 3, 2007. http://www.sandhill.com/opinion/daily_blog.php?id=27&post=367.
4. Anirban Dutta, "6 Great Tips to Do Business with Americans," *Rediff News*, July 6, 2006. http://in.rediff.com/money/2006/jul/06guest2.htm.

5. Mahan Khalsa and Randy Illig, *Let's Get Real or Let's Not Play: Transforming the Buyer/Seller Relationship,* 1st ed. (West Valley City, UT: Franklin Covey, 1999).

6. Anirban Dutta, "How to Beat Dirty Negotiating Tactics—10 Tips," *Rediff News,* August 17, 2007. http://www.rediff.com/money/2007/aug/17bspec.htm.

CHAPTER 10

Case Study

A Real-Life Example of a Service Provider Pursuing Strategic Deals

In the previous chapters, we discussed the tools and methodologies needed for pursuing and winning Big Deals. It is one thing to understand these methods and practices, but another thing to apply them in the context of a large organization, align the divisions, and create the right synergy in order to be effective in winning large deals. The objective of this chapter is to outline a real-life example and show how a service provider pursued large and strategic deals.

But before we can jump into the *how*, we have to understand the basics of this service provider's organizational structure.[1]

A Crash Course in Service Provider's Organization Structure

Customer

Figure 10.1 shows that the customer is in the center of this service provider's organization structure. The organization revolves around *"servicing"* the customer with double delight. The organization structure is designed to create optimum value for the customer through the best service, be it via furnishing total cost of ownership (TCO) reduction, innovation, or other types of value optimization.

Vertical Business Units

The vertical business units depicted in the top part of Figure 10.1 are the engine behind this organization's service orientation for the customer. The VBUs are the industry-facing business units. This service provider offers services for more than 20 industries, including all the usual suspects such as telecoms, banking, insurance, and

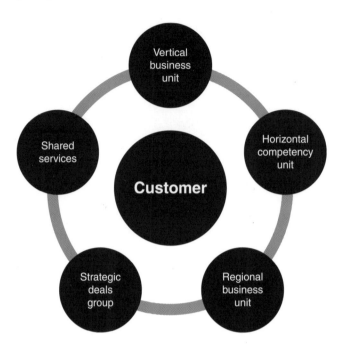

Figure 10.1 Service Provider's Service-Oriented Organizational Architecture

automotive. The VBUs are globally responsible for creating industry-specific solutions for the customer. An example of such a solution would be creation of payroll-specific processes for a particular industry that can be customized for all customers in the same industry. The VBUs also create service offerings, designed to package three facets of service creation: (1) deciphering customer needs to create meaningful technical and business requirements, (2) integrating technology enablers to fulfill those requirements by turning service creation into a finite solution, and (3) creating a mechanism that takes the solution to market. For most large accounts (generating US$5 million in revenue per year or more), the executive managing the account is also from the VBU. In addition to the core services mentioned before, VBUs engage in presales and sales activities for all customers in the United States.

Regional Business Units (RBUs)

Opposite the VBUs in Figure 10.1, you see the circle called regional business units (RBUs). The organization currently has three RBUs in place, one to support Europe, one for Asia, and a third for all of the Americas except the United States. The RBUs are primarily responsible for business development, sales, and presales in these regions. RBUs bring local language and culture skills, regional influences, ethnic staff, and other specific regionalized skill sets that are crucial to winning deals in each region. In short, the RBUs act as the sales force for multiple VBUs within a particular region. The RBUs manage the accounts, from an account and program management perspective, until they generate US$5 million in revenue per year, at which point the VBUs take over these responsibilities. The VBUs, being bigger in size, have more resource bandwidth to manage these larger accounts.

Horizontal Competency Units (HCUs)

The horizontal competency units (HCUs) are the BUs responsible for technology delivery. HCUs include application development and support, SAP, and engineering services. These competencies are the services that the VBUs and RBUs sell to the customer. All the professionals who actually do the delivery of the work, such as writing code, come from this group.

Shared Services (SSUs)

The SSUs are also called support services units. These are the groups that "serve" the typical business and administrative needs of this organization. These units include human resources (HR), finance, legal, marketing, and other administrative support groups.

Strategic Deals Group (SDG)

The strategic deals group is a hybrid of the SSUs and HCUs but also a group that is directly measured by revenue growth or top-line target. So even though SDG is a support unit, it acts as a profit center. SDG teams up with a BU champion (a senior leader in a VBU or RBU) and together they create the interaction among organizational units in Big Deal pursuits. This is to ensure that the best possible integrated solutions are crafted to meet the customer's sourcing drivers and expected business outcomes. SDG also carries out such other functions as research, TPA liaison, contract negotiations, management of risk on the deal, knowledge management, and partner or teammate selections, rounding out overall offerings.

Now that you have a fair idea of the organizational structure, it will be easy to showcase how a deal team (also called a bid team) operates across this structure.

The Deal Pursuit Process: Putting Service Orientation into Practice

We have shared, in the earlier chapters, how a company can find large global sourcing deals. This section highlights what happens when a deal is found or initiated. In nine out of 10 scenarios, deal initiation is an invitation from the customer to present an outline of a proposed solution. The customer may be seeking a detailed response by issuing an RFP or seeking a high-level response by releasing an RFI. Typically, the relationship manager or partner deployed in an account gets the invitation from the customer to participate in the bidding process. Immediately, a core bid team is formed. Sometimes there are no RFPs or RFIs. In such instances, the relationship manager identifies the opportunity by having proactive dialogues with the customer. This is the ideal scenario for us as service providers, because we should face less competition, at least theoretically.

The core team is formed at the outset of the deal. This team consists of the relationship manager from the VBU or RBU, the deal director from the SDG, a solution-office leader, a delivery head from the HCU, and a financial strategist. These team members follow a structured pursuit process that helps in navigating through the bidding steps. The optimized pursuit process consists of six steps, from opportunity identification to deal debrief. The process is described here and in Figure 10.2.

Stage 1	Stage 2	Stage 3	Stage 4	Stage 5	Stage 6
Opportunity review and qualification	Pursuit strategy development	Solution development and pricing	Evaluation and due diligence	Contract negotiation	Deal debrief

Figure 10.2 Service Provider's Pursuit Process Architecture

- *Stage One: opportunity review and qualification* A vetting process to evaluate the service provider's chances of winning the deal before investing in time, money, and resources
- *Stage Two: pursuit strategy development* The process of creating the win plan and central theme for the pursuit
- *Stage Three: solution development and pricing* The process of creating the technical and financial proposal
- *Stage Four: evaluation and due diligence* A thorough review to validate winning factors such as proposal, pricing, and solution
- *Stage Five: contract negotiation* Service provider and the customer work out the contract to come to a mutually acceptable position
- *Stage Six: deal debrief* Capturing the lessons learned for continuous improvement of the organization

Stage 1: Opportunity Review and Qualification	
Step	Activity
1	Collect opportunity information regarding customer, stakeholders, competitors, etc.
2	Assess customer's financial stability to pay for services rendered.
3	Understand opportunity size, contract period, relationship status with customer.
4	Preassess if this opportunity is worth bidding.
5	Solicit support from verticals, horizontals, and support units.
6	Formulate high-level pursuit plan.
7	Conduct initial gate review and do pursuit deal debrief.

Note: This stage requires high participation from the deals team.

Figure 10.3   Matrix for Opportunity Review and Evaluation

Stage One: Opportunity Review and Qualification

The architecture of integrated solutions starts at the opportunity review and qualification phase by defining the set of parameters, standards, and competencies required to meet the customer's needs (see Figure 10.3). Basically, this initial phase evaluates the opportunity. Big Deals require the involvement of many people working from multiple HCUs, VBUs, and RBUs, across borders. In other words, it can be expensive to bid. It is critical to ensure that the bid is worth it for this organization. The deal team thoroughly studies the requirements, with the help of solution experts, to come up with a go-no-go strategy. If the team feels

Stage 2: Pursuit Strategy Development	
Step	Activity
1	Set up deal pursuit program office.
2	Map service provider's capabilities with competitors' capabilities.
3	Determine customer's service provider evaluation criteria.
4	Create deal strategy for win theme, partnership, pricing, competition, and solution.
5	Obtain appropriate budget to pursue bid.
6	Create pursuit plan.
7	Conduct gate review to validate strategy.

Note: This stage requires high participation from the deals team.

Figure 10.4   Matrix for Pursuit Strategy Development

that there is enough business reasoning and a good chance to win this deal, they decide to move forward.

Stage Two: Pursuit Strategy Development

Although the core team anchors the pursuit, the pursuit is won by contributions from many people (see Figure 10.4). The deal director, along with the help of the VBU, creates a program office and assigns a bid manager to run the pursuit. This bid manager is effectively a project manager who organizes the daily work breakdown structures and holds people accountable for delivery. The main thrust of this stage, besides setting up the project management office, is to create a rough solution. The definition of a rough solution, in practice, is loose. In some rare cases, bid teams are actually able to put a first draft of the solution in place. One of the most vital parts of this process, if it is carried out right, is to estimate the resource and technology needs so that a rough pricing draft can be pulled together. But in reality, most of the time bid teams at this organization do not get this far at this stage. They mainly generate similar proposals, have discussions with HCU subject matter experts, and concoct a "back of the envelope" guess of the resource and technology needs and associated pricing. Good deal teams are able to come up with a "win theme" by this point. Win themes are true value differentiators that help win the deal. A win theme is a point-by-point solution set with clear differentiators pegged to the customers' key objectives.

Stage 3: Solution Development and Pricing	
Step	Activity
1	Develop solution, proposal, and supporting collateral.
2	Build pricing models and finalize risk analysis.
3	Lead redlining of contractual documents.
4	Provide solution in the proposal.
5	Obtain appropriate internal reviews to submit bid.

Note: This stage requires selective participation from the deals team.

Figure 10.5 Matrix for Solution Development and Pricing

Stage Three: Solution Development and Pricing

This is the heart of the proposal response, where the actual proposed solution is written in print, work estimates such as delivery times and equipment needs are clearly defined, and a price tag is put in place (see Figure 10.5). The financial (or pricing) strategist plays a key role in coming up with creative pricing options. Big Deals are won or lost on the basis of pricing innovation. Creativity, such as volume discounting, arm-twisting product vendors to get better software and hardware rates, and using shared resources with other deals, becomes critical in winning the deal and making it profitable.

A Big Deals solution development exercise is complex, and the deal solution architecture needs to be modular yet well integrated. Some of the solution components making up this architecture are described here:

- *Technical solution* While evaluating the technical solution, it is imperative to portray how this organization plans to address the global sourcing objectives of the customer. You must ensure not only that the HCUs are delivering the solutions correctly but also that the holistic solution, across technologies, is integrated appropriately.
- *Transition solution* As demonstrated in Chapter Eleven, transition is one of the most critical areas of global sourcing. Ironing out how service delivery will be transferred from the customer to this service provider is the key focus of this section.
- *HR solution* A big part of many Big Deals is employee rebadging. The deal team works closely with the HR unit to ensure that the transitioned employees are a fit for this organization. The HR team goes through a detailed process to ensure culture and competency fit.

- *Transformation and value-adds* The key addition in this phase is to pin down how service delivery is transformed to enhance greater strategic value-adds for the customer.
- *Contracts* In this phase of contract definition, the service provider gives enough clarity in MSAs, LSAs, and other contractual and related operational documents to ensure that this service provider and customers are on the same page.
- *Financial and pricing solution* This is really all about deal structuring. Financial strategists along with solution architects work diligently to ensure that the optimum pricing model and financial structure are in place that will help reach a win-win position with the customer.
- *Risk-management plan* Our interviews with CIOs showed us that managing risk is probably the most essential concern for them. Here the service provider proposes risk-management and mitigation procedures on two levels: assessing risk (via quantitative models such as Monte Carlo analysis) and mitigating that risk with operational risk-management procedures.
- *Assumptions* Assumptions are the key to the architecture of the solution. Many of the fixed bids become profitable because assumptions reflect customer-solution realities. Solution teams spend a lot of time understanding and explaining assumptions to customers.
- *Governance solution* Last but not least, it is critical to clearly demonstrate how the work is going to be governed. Assurance regarding governance and accountability from the operations and project level all the way to the executive level is detailed out here.

Typically, the solution architecture is created by a cross-functional team (see Figure 10.6) drawn from various collaborating circles.

This team examines various "solution influencers" to design the sourcing solution. For every line item, deal makers ask themselves several searching questions. The goal of this exercise is to be completely comfortable with the prescribed approach to the customer.

All the terms and conditions on such benchmarks as price ceilings and hours of work ceilings are documented in the contract, that is, the MSA. Basically, the MSA outlines such matters as penalties, term violation procedures, and escalation mechanisms. MSAs are pure legalese. In accounts where this service provider maintains a good relationship with the customer, the MSA never sees the light of day. However, should things go south, MSAs will help bring clarity in terms of what course of action to take. Needless to say, the SDG financial

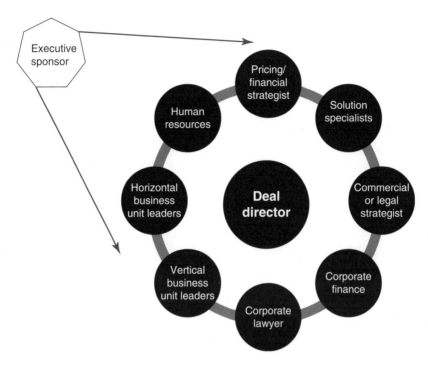

Figure 10.6   Service Provider's Pursuit Team Architecture

strategist (sometimes called the pricing or commercial strategist) works closely with the legal department to ensure that the terms and conditions are acceptable. Normally, this organization takes the customer-provided MSA, makes changes based on the goal and agenda, and sends it back to the customer. This MSA is negotiated in a later step.

This service provider, like others, actively tries to engage with multiple units of the customer organization at this time to get customer- and deal-specific intelligence. Mainly, this is done via backdoor diplomacy. Use of existing customers, partners, and suppliers to broker those meetings is a common thing. Knowing who the competitors are is helpful, as well as knowing who, in the customer organization, is opposed to or championing global sourcing. It is imperative to discover the true global sourcing business drivers (those supplied in the RFI or RFP may not be accurate, or in many cases they are incomplete). This step also validates whether a TPA is going to help the customer make the decision. If this is the case, the game plan should reflect it. To make a long story short: stage three is the one that defines the success or failure of the deal.

Stage 4: Evaluation and Due Diligence	
Step	Activity
1	Prepare proposal defense.
2	Present proposal and address questions raised about it.
3	Resubmit proposal with best and final offer after customer feedback.
4	Plan and prepare for due diligence.
5	Arrange site visits and customer references.
6	Conduct reviews, deal qualification, and pursuit team debrief.

Note: This stage requires selective participation from the deals team.

Figure 10.7   Matrix for Evaluation and Due Diligence

Stage Four: Evaluation and Due Diligence

It is a great achievement by itself to reach this stage. It means the organization has at least made the customer's shortlist. This stage is also loosely defined because customers can call this organization for a proposal defense (see Figure 10.7). The proposal defense could be one meeting or a series of meetings where the customer visits this service provider's delivery centers and interviews the people who will work on the account. Customers also spend a lot of time quizzing service provider leaders about specific risk-management strategies, backup plans, and domain knowledge. They want to ensure that they have a thorough understanding of all proposals from every provider before proceeding with the final selection decision.

Stage 5: Contract Negotiations	
Step	Activity
1	Draft contract terms and conditions.
2	Finalize partnership and teaming arrangements.
3	Determine negotiation strategy, and prioritize positions.
4	Role-play negotiations.
5	Lead negotiation and finalize contracts (MSA, LSA etc.).
6	Summarize opportunity outcome, and create win-loss report.

Note: This stage requires high participation from the deals team.

Figure 10.8   Matrix for Contract Negotiations

Stage Five: Contract Negotiation

Remember the MSA from stage three? We discuss it in detail here (see Figure 10.8). The customer has agreed in principle to work with this organization at this point. Rarely do they drag two or three vendors to this stage and pit them against each other. The SDG financial strategist (in collaboration with corporate finance) takes the lead at this point and works with the BU leaders from the VBUs and the HCUs, along with the customer business leaders, to reach a win-win scenario. This service provider and the customer both want to get it done at this point, so typically, after some hard- and soft-balling, both sides reach a consensus. Then, once the contract is signed, the Champagne bottle is opened!

Stage 6: Deal Debrief	
Step	Activity
1	Conduct internal debrief with pursuit team.
2	Participate in prospect decision debrief.
3	Communicate deal results to all service provider stakeholders.
4	Close out the pursuit program office.
5	Turn over deal-related documents to knowledge management team.

Note: This stage requires high participation from the deals team.

Figure 10.9 Matrix for Deal Debrief

Stage Six: Deal Debrief

SDG deal directors are required to hold meetings to review what went well and what did not work, regardless of whether the deal is won or not (see Figure 10.9). So step six is mandatory. Although this organization got better in capturing these lessons while we were there, it is still far from calling itself successful in this aspect. Deal teams tend to disappear quickly at this stage, to work on other deals.

Summary

The service-oriented architecture for pursuits helps optimize the high investment effort typically associated with large global sourcing solutions. This approach also ensures that the right expertise is brought forward from the right service provider BUs, to the right customer stakeholder, at the right time in the process.

Note

1. Sandeep Srivastava and Hetzel Folden, "Satyam's Strategic Pursuit Service Oriented Architecture for Offering Global Sourcing Solutions," *Satyam Technology Review*, January 2008, pages 1-4.

SECTION IV

MANAGING DEALS

CHAPTER 11

Managing Transitions and Change

The Stepping Stones for Delivering Service

Transition management is often underestimated when doing large deals. You may also be wondering, "What does this have to do with winning and closing large deals?" In our view, successful deal closures are not hit-and-run new business capture events. Winning Big Deals is a strategic process that includes *keeping the deal closed.*

Many service providers give a lot of thought to winning the deal and managing the deal. But too often they naïvely believe that just because they have a transition management document in place, there should be little problem following that document when doing transitions. The reality is that transitions play a crucial role in how the future state of service delivery will look in a particular account. Good transitions help build not only good delivery framework within the account but also customer confidence in the incoming service provider.

Service providers can learn a lesson about the value of transitions from American politics. Right after November 4, 2008, the day of the U.S. presidential election, the media was flooded with information about how Barack Obama, then president-elect, was creating a transition plan immediately after winning the vote. He had learned from the Clinton administration that a delayed or seemingly sloppy transition can create a lot of hurdles right from the implementation get-go. History tells us how Bill Clinton faced a lot of opposition and criticism in his first years, which many believe was due to a relatively poor transition. Well, Obama's transition was not smooth as silk either, but he did try to do a good job and pay special attention to transition.

The First Course in Transition

Transition, in the context of outsourcing service delivery, is the transfer of service delivery responsibility from the client (or from an incumbent service delivery provider) to the incoming service delivery provider.

The responsibilities for delivering certain artifacts or services are covered under a new, modified, or expanded contract. The service provider is expected to put a governance structure in place that will help manage the transition into a steady state. The customer's employees are expected to learn new competencies and work alongside the new service provider. New ways of sharing information, managing risks, and measuring performance are put in place. Finally, clear transition entry and exit criteria need to be defined so that service providers and customers can judge the success of the transition.

A best practice for the client and service provider personnel is to jointly conduct a contract debrief of the requirements and obligations of both parties, agreed during the bid and negotiation process. This joint debrief can then also facilitate joint transition planning, as discussed later in the chapter.

Making smooth, seamless transitions is much easier if there is a "memory" from closing the deal to executing the transition. This often includes the transition manager, who was also on the pursuit team (see Box 11.1). If that is not possible, then a formal handover meeting should occur. The pursuit team highlights the deliverables of transition and the risks, allowing the transition manager to ask questions and fully understand the role.

Box 11.1: When Continuity Fails, Relationships Sour

Hetzel recalls a deal where the contract was concluded and a formal handover occurred. However, six months into transition the entire leadership of the service provider's transition team changed. These changes occurred because of an inadequate supply of transition leaders. As a result, the transition milestones were missed; the client became extremely unhappy and proceeded to escalate the issues through the executive steering committee, threatening a termination-for-cause. As all parties scurried to baseline the transition deliverables once again, Hetzel volunteered to work with both sides. He was in a good position to reset the deliverables because he was the one continuous link from the original deal negotiations. As the "honest broker," he facilitated restructuring the transition plan to the satisfaction of both parties, and ultimately the new plan

(continued)

produced successful deliveries. The key to this success was continuity from the contract closure. Deal groups should incorporate the philosophy that if they supported the deal, they should be available, throughout the relationship, to assist in any additional activities.

There are four aspects to global sourcing transitions. However, not all of them have to be present for the process to be called a global sourcing transition.

- *Service transition* This is the most common type of transition. All customers understand that a set of services will now be delivered by the new service provider. These services could be the creation of new artifacts or maintaining existing services. Service transitions may also include transferring physical and intellectual assets such as buildings and intellectual property to the service provider.
- *People transfer* People transfer, which is also called rebadging, is a mechanism by which the customer transfers a bunch of their employees to the service provider's payroll. In Chapter Six, we discussed the contractual part of this transfer under the pricing model. But outside of the contract, there is a huge operational effort that must take place to pull off a transfer. Managing logistics, employee documentation, and most important, morale, are the biggest challenges.
- *Commercial transition* Most of the time, new work will entail changing commercial terms. Sometimes, new work comes under the existing MSA clause, where no new commercial terms are created to deliver the new work. Commercial transition highlights change in commercial agreement.
- *Organizational transition* Organizational transition is always present in all new service-delivery engagements. The customer organization is always affected one way or the other. Change management plays a major role in organization transition.

Service providers should have a two-pronged strategy to make transitions successful. First, they need to craft an effective transition implementation framework. We believe there should be at least five distinct stages within the framework. Second, they must ensure customer partnership and support during transition. Next we explain the transition implementation framework depicted in Figure 11.1.

Figure 11.1 Service Delivery Transition Framework

Preplan
- Study retained and sourced organization.
- Initiate change management agenda with customer

Deal closing

Plan
- Start knowledge transfer.
- Transfer assets, people, etc.
- Analyze business and technical architecture.

Service provider starts work

Implement
- Seek issue-free work using customer's "as is" processes.
- Implement change management process.
- Redesign technology architecture.

Service starts

Transform
- Service provider implements technical, functional, and organizational change.

Service provider transforms

Steady state
- Perform in new "as is" state.
- Continuously improve by changing resource mix and utilization ratio.

Service provider finishes work

Preplan

Service providers seriously thinking about excelling in the transition process should start planning transition early in the game. It's true that it is often impossible to get a good feel for what will happen during a transition because the details about service delivery are unavailable. But it is our duty, as service providers, to encourage our customers to talk through transition-specific points during contract negotiation and signing. It is our job to educate the customers' understanding that the shape of the transition can seriously affect deal costs and future service delivery. Also, if the transition is preplanned, service providers can start planning as soon as the deal closes. Good planning will also help manage change, which is discussed later in the chapter. It is in our best interest as well to put clearly defined and measurable transition entry and exit points in the contract so there can be no ambiguity on what we delivered and how well.

Plan

This is the core stage within the framework. The provider should actively study the customer organization from a high level and understand what is being retained and what is being outsourced. Several onsite people from the service provider should be deployed on the customer's premises to start the work. Service providers should undergo both formal and informal knowledge-transfer (KT) activities during this phase. If the engagement requires people or asset transfer, this is the stage where it should take place.

Implement

The main goal of the implementation stage is to deliver issue-free service by keeping customer processes "as is." However, while supporting the customer, the service provider should break down the proposed work into easily understood chunks of work packages. The work packages should clearly define service levels. Customers are often used to grouping projects together and may not use a service-delivery model where resources are optimized. Service providers need to start working as quickly as possible to understand the existing application architecture. David Hott is a solutions architect with IBM who has been a key player in several large deal transitions. He proposes that the provider-side solution architects should quickly evaluate the existing customer architecture and assess how it will fit within a standardized application software development process such as the rational unified process. This approach to understanding applications helps optimize service delivery models further down the road. David's advice is applicable even if you are simply contracted for pure support work and not transformation work. Understanding the architectural optimization gap can eventually become a selling point for business transformation.

Transform

This stage is the reason customers really outsource. The work is well understood by the service provider, and existing SLAs are already being met. The design team has also analyzed the business and process gaps. This is where new business and supporting technical architectures are implemented to increase efficiency and offer optimization. This stage generally comes after a few months of pure as-is support.

Steady State

The work is delivered in the new as-is stage. In an ideal scenario, the bulk of the work should have been transferred to the offshore locations and the delivery teams should have taken full control of performing the work.

The Essential Element in Transition: Join Your Customer at the Hip

The second part of a successful transition is the customer partnership. In many global sourcing deals, senior executives in the customer community make the call on outsourcing work. Many operational rank-and-file employees actually go into work hoping and praying that the deal fails. As a result, many customers, at the operational level, are not willing or interested in actively participating in the transition. As a new service provider, you have to build relationships quickly at the project level so that your customer helps you gather information about existing system knowledge and documentation. Your customers also need to help you with coordinating customer KT interviews (for example, lunch-and-learn sessions) so that you can acquire the relevant knowledge.

The service provider transition manager and the customer's dedicated resource should be joined at the hip and work toward a shared outcome. There should be a clear directive on what is expected from the customer as far as transition help is concerned.

Mahesh Ramachandran has been given many titles. He has been called a project manager, a lead analyst, and even a domain quality expert. Mahesh has been an active part of several small- and large-scale project transitions for a major telecom business. He has worked closely with two huge global service providers and a few small service providers in this process over the last seven years. He has also been an active participant in a reverse transition where some of the work allocated to service providers was brought back because of lack of success. In short, he is experienced in global sourcing transitions from the customer side.

His main job at this telecom customer, regardless of the title, is, as he put it, "getting work done from the service providers." We requested his thoughts on what a service provider should do to have a good partnership with the customer during transition. Here is his unique perspective for service providers.

- *Coach them right* Many customer employees are experts in working in their own domains. But they are not current on the latest industry best practices and terminologies. So it is hard for these employees to truly understand service provider terms and frameworks. The service provider needs to work closely with the customer program manager (or somebody who is assigned at the project level to help the service provider) to create a glossary of terms. But outside of creating the glossary, the customer employees must be coached on the entire transition process in simple terms, so that the success measures are well understood.
- *Demand respect* This is an interesting point that came from Mahesh, who has spent his entire career in a customer organization. He noticed that many service provider employees, especially those brought in from offshore to do quick knowledge transfer, react passively when customers do not show them respect. Service providers need to push back disrespectful behavior as early as possible. This sets the tone of the partnership and results in more respectful sharing of information in the days to come.

- *Seek customer executive intervention* If a service provider fails to get information during the knowledge transfer phase because somebody in the customer community is road blocking, it is critical for the service provider to raise it as an issue with the customer executive team. Service providers tend to escalate less because doing so shows an inability to manage. However, escalating early a few times also sets the right tone for the service-delivery transition.
- *Thorough transition focus* Service providers should quickly get a grip on the existing customer environment. There are a few musthaves that need to be put in place as part of a detailed transition plan. All large deals require dedicated use of a transition manager. It is imperative to cue the transition manager in to the project management office right away. The customer should also be persuaded to dedicate a full-time resource to help out in transition.

Managing Change: We Can and We Must

Much of what we have discussed so far affects customer employees, who are expected to change behavior. Service providers need to play the role of change managers during and beyond transition. Employees who are absolutely furious because the service provider took jobs away from their former colleagues, or employees who are forcibly being retooled, are all part of the change-affected community. Dealing with change dynamics in people should be a systematic effort. This effort should start early in the transition phase, where the participants of this discussion are the leadership teams of both the service provider and the customer. The effort should include processes for dealing with change. The processes should be applicable at all levels of the affected customer organization. The change management process requires data gathering, analysis, planning, and implementation. It should be based on true assessment of the customer's history, readiness, and capacity to adapt culturally. The process should be integrated into the transition plan and later passed on to the program governance plan.

However, all change management efforts will fail if service providers cannot deal with people. As you have noticed, the overwhelming theme of this book has been on building relationships at all levels. Today's customer may be tomorrow's colleague. We strongly believe that service providers should train their employees to build good relationships with the customer at all levels. Although dealing with the soft side of human relationships is not a new concept, we "left brainers" like to believe that we can quantifiably solve all these issues through documents, measures, and metrics. We need to remind ourselves, as service providers, that as much as metrics, benchmarks, and processes matter, we are dealing with human beings who have emotions and value relationships.

But before we go too deep into understanding change in lieu of outsourcing, here is a story about Ken Green (see Box 11.2).

Box 11.2: The Story of Ken Green

Ken Green, from Dallas, is a 20-year veteran in the active reserve of the U.S. Air Force. In the summer of 2008, he was deployed to the Persian Gulf as an officer. He was in charge of managing logistics and the supply chain for the Iraq War as well as supporting troops deployed in the Horn of Africa. He and his team were tasked with refueling, maintaining, and repairing war planes flying in and out of the Iraqi and Djibouti skies. Logistics management had to be picture-perfect, as the planes were manicured mid-air under extreme time restrictions. Ken's team had to ensure that planes carrying oil, supplies, and support staff were on hand to service these planes the moment they arrived on deck. The planning also included replenishing these supplies so that there was zero deviation from allocated service times. The Air Force manages every move as a metric, so any deviation is a measure unmet.

But this logistics support role also had another unadvertised component in it, the component of managing change. For example, Ken was the person who had to make calls on how to handle a situation when a junior team member of his unit could not change the oil of a plane waiting in the air hangar. This was because he had become depressed after hearing that his house in Florida had been foreclosed while he was deployed. Or the time when another of his younger troopers grabbed a fellow soldier by the neck in extreme rage because his wife back home in Mississippi was having an affair. Ken's *mantra* for managing these occurrences of daily mayhem: "Stay calm and think clear."

For the past 20 years, when he is not deployed he has also maintained a parallel corporate career as a technology manager. So it's no surprise that his present employer, Accenture, often

(continued)

decides to assign Ken as a transition manager in their most strategic deals. Transition management is as much about having a process as it is about dealing with change. And who can manage change better than somebody like Ken, who has managed grown men who cry like babies and fight like crazy pit bulls?

The good thing is that we don't all have to experience what Ken has been through in combat in order to manage change. All of us can learn to manage change, just as Obama said in his presidential campaign tagline of "change we can believe in." Over the years we have experienced change dynamics in many large global sourcing transitions. We have seen what works and what does not. We have compiled below what we believe are the essential ingredients of change management processes for large service delivery.[1]

Start High, Then Go Deep and Wide

The change agenda should start at the top and disseminate to all parts of the organization. Change is an unsettling experience. To alleviate some of the discomfort caused by change, it is critical to involve customer leadership in promoting change. In almost all cases, wherever we see customer executives take a leadership role in facilitating change, adjusting to change goes a lot more smoothly for customers. Customers feel comforted if their senior executives embrace the new entrant (the service provider) and help create a collaborative environment. As a service provider, we need to encourage, and if necessary force, the customer executives to be change champions. Anirban remembers an entire customer leadership team going behind the curtains as the service provider came in. No one wanted to be the bad guy by embracing the service provider in front of the rank-and-file team. The result was dismal. After a terrible transition, which had hostile customers not sharing information, the service provider failed to deliver most of the promised value as it encountered hostility all the way. After a year, the private equity firm that owned part of the customer business forced some senior customer executives out and literally bulldozed the collaboration. As a service provider, you do not want to see that happen in your customer organization.

It's also important to realize that global sourcing affects every part of the organization. This includes those not currently using outsourcing.

Employees fear that their jobs will go next. Service providers need to work with customers so that the change agenda trickles down into all the nooks and crannies of the customer organization. Basically, the change agenda should convey that the company cares for its employees, is doing what is best for the shareholders, and is going to do everything possible to ensure that employees are taken care of. Customer executives should create a mechanism (with the help of the service provider if needed) to disseminate change management training at all levels. An executive can train 10 directors, who in turn can train 50 managers. In every part of the organization, the managers who are identified and trained must be aligned to the company's vision of global sourcing, ready to execute their specific mission, and anxious to make change happen.

Culture-Smart

Many service providers follow a cookie-cutter approach to managing change. What works for one customer does not necessarily work for another. For large customers, different parts of the organization have their own subcultures. The customer organization may be a result of several acquired or merged companies where the existing cultures of the past organizations prevailed. This is also true for geographically distributed customers, where each country or province may have its own cultural flavor.

Cultural sensitivity analysis is a big part of the change management process. Service providers need to work with customers to assess customer organization culture at all levels. The diagnostics must take into consideration the core values, beliefs, behaviors, and perceptions of these individual communities. Once the culture is understood, service providers need to influence customers to create a new business culture (see Box 11.3).

Overcommunicate Rather Than Undercommunicate

We cannot tell you how many times we have seen customers and service providers shy away from communicating global sourcing developments to customer organizations. It is vital to remind customers that if they are not communicating, somebody else is doing it for them. The "somebody else" is, typically, the rumor mill, which promotes

---

Box 11.3: Cultural Assessment: Please Don't Take It for Granted!

About 10 years ago, a famous global service provider got a lucrative sourcing deal in China. The customer was a small Chinese technology company. Chinese customers were few and far between in those days, and no one knew a whole lot about the behavioral patterns of such outfits. The service provider studied Chinese culture thoroughly and equipped its people to deal with the employees. The service provider's account team was gung ho about capitalizing on the concept of *guanxi*. Guanxi is a network of cooperative relationships among multiple parties which basically promotes the philosophy "You scratch my back and I'll scratch yours." A few months into the deal, the service provider realized that the customers were actually mocking their seriousness about following Chinese business culture. On further investigation, it was discovered that most of the leadership team of this product manufacturing company had grown up in the San Francisco Bay Area. Although Chinese by race, they were Americans by behavior. These young entrepreneurs took pride in shaping a business culture that was downright Yankee in nature. In this case, the service provider's valiant efforts in aligning them with a foreign culture simply backfired.

---

negative vibes all the way through the customer organization. We strongly urge service providers to partner with customers in clearly defining change items and plans to implement them. The core change message should be presented often, through various channels. Erring on the side of overcommunication is much safer than undercommunicating in this circumstance. The message delivery should be inspirational, with some sales spin in it. Communication should be a multi-way device. Employees at all levels in the customer organization should be able to clarify their doubts and even furnish inputs to the global sourcing initiative.

Think on Your Feet (Be Flexible)

We can assure you that no matter how hard you try, your change process will encounter unexpected hindrances. People react unexpectedly, as in the story of the Chinese business people told in Box 11.3. External environments also change behaviors. We have seen that, immediately after September 11, 2001, many customer employees who had passive racist feelings started voicing them more aggressively. People started to unfairly clump terrorist action with foreigners working at their premises. Service providers championing change management should continuously assess the organization's mood and adapt accordingly. The assessment should be based on both quantitative and qualitative data from the customer organization.

Conclusion

Transition and change go hand in hand. Our effort in this chapter was to give you a basic understanding of what is needed to be successful in managing transition and change. Even if all your frameworks and processes regarding transition and change management come up short, a genuine interest in doing well for the customer, coupled with the desire to really build friendships with them, will help you manage change and transition.

Note

1. John Jones, DeAnne Aguirre, and Matthew Calderone, "10 Principles of Change Management," *Strategy + Business*, April 15, 2004. http://www.strategy-business.com/resilience/rr00006?pg=0.

CHAPTER 12

Managing Integrated Programs

A Practical Take on Service Delivery Governance

It's never been more critical for technology service providers to truly understand their customers' need to get work done. Today, the global economy is in the tank and hopes for full recovery are nowhere in sight. Under these economic conditions, it is an absolute must that technology service providers bring world-class processes and procedures to make every big delivery successful. A major delivery failure is guaranteed to flush both the customer and the provider into oblivion. In Chapter One, we echoed tennis player and successful entrepreneur Mahesh Bhupathi's motto of building customer relationships that are based on reliable delivery of outcomes. Well, furnishing dependable technology service delivery is the biggest reliability test a service provider can give a customer in order to sustain a long-term business relationship.

But delivering Big Deals is not easy. Customers are geographically spread and are also engaged in a faster-than-ever rat race to deliver their end results. To be successful in Big Deals delivery, service providers need to look at service delivery in a completely different way from how they viewed it before. To make large-deal service delivery a step better than yesterday, though, you need to understand the pitfalls of managing global outsourcing delivery via the traditional model.

The Shortcomings of the Traditional Globally Sourced Service Delivery Model

If you look at the last 10 years, you will see that most large service providers used a two-pronged approach to manage Big Deals service delivery via the onsite-offshore model. They believed in passing the buck and "throwing the work over the pond" as approaches to managing their customers' work (see Box 12.1).

Box 12.1: Global Delivery Gone Bad: Lessons from a Telecom Giant

Although Terrence Shaw is the CEO of a software outfit called Wirevibe today, life for him has not always been so great. Around 10 years ago, he was working for a major telecom company. He moved fast up the totem pole, working all the way from software developer through functional lead, to eventually take charge as IT service delivery manager. Much to his dismay, his company, like its peers, decided to outsource both new development and support of IT services. After many months of negotiation and deliberation, a big outsourcing contract was awarded to two large IT service-delivery providers. Unlike many of the customer employees who were let go, Terrence was offered a position overseeing the delivery work of these two global sourcing giants. He was supposed to be the bridge between the service providers and the customer. The organization had never done any large-scale outsourcing before. They gave Terrence the critical responsibility of helping them get accustomed to the big bad world of global sourcing.

The telecom work the customer did was both complex and customized in many cases. The organization was used to breaking up the work by telecom-specific functional domains rather than technological domains. To the shock of many employees of this customer, both the service providers came in and were eager to break the work into chunks of technology domains rather than keeping it in its functional domains. However, what was shocking for many at the customer site was not really shocking news to some of us. The service providers, in this case, proposed a common horizontally focused delivery model, where the technologically focused teams (horizontals) take the lead and break the work into logical chunks. So the SAP team is responsible for SAP delivery and support, mainframe people are responsible for all things "green screen," and the application development guys will be coding away till the cows come home.

This time-tested, horizontally focused, distributed development methodology works fine for medium-sized deals. In this

(continued)

case, it was a tremendous disaster. Terrence soon realized that although there was a program manager in place at both service providers, they were really viewed by their own employers as nothing more than pencil pushers. One of the service providers called this person an onsite coordinator and the other referred to the role as program lead. The commonality was that both of them had no real power except taking status from the multiple project managers and doing escalations to their own management sitting overseas. Basically, the program manager took the work and, along with a couple of onsite cohorts, simply threw the work over the pond. The two service providers did most of their work from India, Brazil, and Argentina, which was where the bulk of their delivery teams resided. Terrence and his team never got to know the project managers well because project management responsibility was always changing hands as work was shifted between multiple technology groups and phases of the services life cycle. Besides, the only interaction between the customer and the offshore team was through long-distance calls and the even more impersonal remote Web-based status reviews.

As a matter of fact, the only time Terrence met two of the project managers, from both the service providers, was during a disaster. A functionality was built, it passed user acceptance testing, and was about to go into production when the customer realized it was missing two major components. If this work had gone into production, the customer would have lost serious money rectifying the consequences. As a result, both service provider executives and delivery heads were summoned to the customer head office for a tongue lashing.

The biggest challenge Terrence faced was when something really difficult came up in production or delivery; there was no real owner. The buck just kept getting passed around, until Terrence and some of the customers' retained architects took control of the situation and helped fix the problem.

Terrence held an executive briefing for the senior members of this telecom outfit. His recommendation included forcing the service providers to change their service-delivery model completely so that the customer enjoys more visibility of the work and also establishing a single overall point of control for the work.

Many service providers like to preach that what Terrence experienced as a customer 10 years ago is the tale of a bygone era. But the reality is that, even today, several service providers try to follow an outdated global sourcing model that lacks accountability and commitment to performance improvement.

What Does the Customer Want from a Service Provider?

Every major service provider works mostly on a globally sourced, service-delivery model. But the difference between the ones who can maximize their efficiency in delivering Big Deals and those who cannot is decided by how well the service provider manages the delivery.

A service provider has three main agendas to satisfy in a customer organization. They belong to the chief financial officer (CFO), the chief information officer (CIO), and the chief operations officer (COO).

The CFO's Agenda

The CFO's focus is on increasing the top line (revenue) and the bottom line (profitability) for the organization. Most service providers zone in on this need of the CFO's, during the bid pursuit process, and try to appease them by showing the possible financial benefits. However, we have seen many service providers, once the project is in motion, shift their energy purely into operations. They tend to limit their thinking about creating financial benefits for the customer. They cease to think of creative ways of continuously appeasing the CFO while the project is in motion. In Chapters Six and Seven, our pricing and deal-structuring chapters, we covered at great length how service providers can structure deals innovatively to help customers' top and bottom lines. Well, deal structuring does not have to stop once the deal is in progress and the contract has been signed. After the account team is engaged, the client partner, program manager, and delivery manager from the service provider should continuously figure out ways to financially add value for the customer by using creative financial techniques. If your team can come up with a better financial model halfway through a project that will save customer money, you had better believe that your customer will be willing to consider it as an amendment to the contract. Whenever you are delivering, our suggestion is to align yourself with the CFO's agenda at all times.

The CIO's Agenda

The CIO, in contrast, prefers to see a service-delivery model that is competent, technology-agnostic, scalable, reliable, and flexible. In most cases, the CIO's head is on the chopping block if the service provider fails to deliver. When we met Tom Halbouty, CIO of Pioneer Resources, we asked him a simple question. What does he specifically look for from a service provider? Tom said that although he is looking for many things that we mention as the CIO wish list from a service provider, his biggest concern is risk. Regardless of who the service delivery provider is, if the risk assessment and mitigation procedures are not battle-tested he shies away from awarding deals to that service provider. Tom, a former engagement leader with a Big Five consulting company, goes on to explain that he liked to see practical governance models that can handle change, risk, and growth effectively. CIOs do not like massive disruption to their technology environment. They understand that the service provider will create some disruption in order to be successful. But for the service provider's service-delivery team to obtain the trust of the CIO, they need to assure the CIO that the service provider's governance mechanism can manage change and handle disruption easily.

The COO's Agenda

Often overlooked by the service providers, the COO makes the vital decisions about the company's business-as-usual agenda. Basically, the BU heads are all part of the COO's office. The COO's office also influences how new divisions need to be glued on (acquisitions) or how old divisions need to be unglued (spin-offs), on the basis of the company's strategic needs. COOs are always interested in how to stretch a dollar—essentially, how to do more with less. Service providers have to ensure that their prime focus is on throughput improvement if they want to appease the COO and make an ally of that person. We talked to Sudhakar Gorti, who held a senior leadership position with operations responsibilities at NBC and Sun Microsystems. Sudhakar has had a storied career of leading many large operations initiatives at multiple Fortune 500 companies, where he has worked with several global service-delivery providers. Sudhakar's pet peeve is that most service providers do not take a leader's role in understanding the existing processes to make them better. They simply focus on delivery excellence by following the existing process or implementing their own process. He believes that understanding process gaps and focusing on optimizing customer processes will help the service providers in truly aligning themselves with the customer. As a service provider, it's imperative that you streamline the existing business processes to optimize delivery.

We have summarized in Table 12.1 many questions that we believe are important to answer if you want to satisfy the needs of all three of your stakeholders: the CFO, the CIO, and the COO.

What's Needed to Manage Big Service-Delivery Engagements: The Collaborative Governance Structure

If we investigate behind-the-scenes footage from the earlier story (Box 12.1) on Terrence's woes with the service provider's attitude of passing the buck and throwing over the pond, we can see that communication failed somewhere. The service providers were not partnering the customer to jointly develop measures and outcomes. Also, the escalation process might have been inadequate; major flags were raised after damage happened. Many customers who have worked successfully in a non-outsourced model have difficulty adjusting to the service provider governance mentality. A common ideology prevails among customers: us versus them. This ideology terms as *us* the customer and as *them* the service provider. This boxed thinking completely destroys the concept of *collaborative governance structure*, which we believe is the key to managing large deliveries.

Collaborative Governance Structure

You do not need fancy charts and maps to run an effective governance program. What you must have is the ability to create an environment where, at every level, the service provider and the customer are working together. We believe that customers should be joined at the hip. Both parties should feel responsible for joint outcomes. The goal is to create camaraderie, at all levels, between the two parties. In simplistic terms, a good governance model should have a number of vital ingredients.

Table 12-1 The C-Level Stakeholder Needs Assessment

Role Focus Area	CFO Finance	CIO Technology Delivery	COO Throughput
Concerns	**1. Profitability**	**1. Relationships**	**1. Integrated alignment**
	Are your delivery teams working creatively to define measures to ensure that the bottom line is improved and that cost overruns are eliminated?	How is your organization ensuring that a good relationship is being built between the customer and your organization?	Does your organization take extra measures to strategically align with your customer's vision, goals, and business objectives?
	How do your account teams allocate resources, people, and artifacts to influence cost cutting and the overall financial success of the deal?	Do you have enough onsite presence, or do you bring in offshore people frequently to meet customers?	How do you continuously ensure that performance is improved technically and functionally on an ongoing basis?
	2. Financial drivers	Are you sure that your end-user satisfaction is well in line with the industry standard?	Are you delivering technology that is aligned with business strategies, tactics, and financial objectives?
	How is your organization reducing ongoing costs for service delivery?	**2. Governance**	**2. Planning**
	Do you have specific metrics for capturing reduction of maintenance costs, reducing integrated development and testing efforts, and increasing the reuse of code, test plans, and test data?	Are your account team members defining the structure, process, and procedure to control customer operations and changes? How is accountability defined?	How does your organization plan to define the performance standards, metrics, and controls that ensure customer success?
	Do you have clear cost visibility and clear identification of all cost drivers?	How do you ensure that your teams cannot pass the buck or "throw it over the pond" when it comes to customer work?	Are the benchmarks your account team is setting comparable to industry best?
	How do you predict costs for services by unit price?		**3. Operational drivers**
			How are you increasing productivity through knowledge retention?

(Continued)

Table 12-1 (Continued)

Role Focus Area	CFO Finance	CIO Technology Delivery	COO Throughput
	On what basis are you estimating cost reductions year-on-year (YOY)?	Does your governance framework involve multiple stakeholders, including business units?	What's your plan for operational quality improvement?
	3. Cost drivers	Are you sharing delivery risks with your customers, using a risk-reward concept?	How do you plan to optimize the effort toward application availability and reducing downtime?
	How are you reducing per-unit costs over the course of the program?	**3. Transformational partnership**	How are you ensuring that you have flexibility built into your supply of services? For example, how do you handle fluctuations in demanded volume, level of service, accessibility to service, and the overall quality and reliability of your effort?
	How are you improving scale at a lower cost base?	Do your long-term goals include productivity targets, value optimization, and continuous improvements?	
		Are you leveraging a multi-shore delivery model on the basis of best value for the customer as opposed to a suitable location for you?	Do you have a plan in place to minimize the risk of service failure in operation of services?
		Are you using your size advantage (if a large service provider) to drive transformation and maintain global best-in-class practices?	Does your team make a constant effort to improve documents so that knowledge can be retained and passed on appropriately?
		Are you re-engineering core processes to create a competitive advantage for your customer?	What is your mechanism to stop fixed-bid overrun?

(Continued)

Are you tightly coupling business needs and outcomes?

4. **Technology drivers**

How are you planning to leverage technology competencies and capabilities from across your organization?

Do you have access to best-in-class, cutting-edge solutions for your services?

How streamlined is your testing and data cleanup process?

How much focus does your team put on overall enterprise systems architecture and planning?

5. **Skills and experience**

Does your organization have access to specialist outside-of-core skills to help your customer's program?

Can you efficiently increase the sourced portion of work overseas to focus on core high-end areas?

4. **Quality**

Are you leveraging best practices and processes to ensure that the quality of work you are delivering improves over time?

Do you have a thorough testing and validation process in place, not just for technical code but for all artifacts (processes, programs)?

Are you providing a single window for all technology requirements?

5. **Customer's competitive challenges**

Will your organization be able to transform its delivery mechanism if your customer goes through a merger or acquisition?

How do you specifically plan to help your customer if it launches a new product or service?

How can you handle a sudden increase in system requirements or capacity?

Executive Sponsors

This group of senior leaders blesses the partnership between the service provider and the customer. The sponsors are not responsible for daily management of outcomes. They approve or reject any major course change or customization. They are also involved in giving strategic guidance. In many ways, this group works like the corporate board of a reputable company. It is imperative to engage top decision makers from both the customer and the service provider in this group. Typically, the group consists of the CIO, the business sponsor (COO or BU head) from the customer side, and a service-provider-side executive, such as a BU head, who is typically at a senior vice president or equivalent level. Our experience with good executive sponsors showed us that this group needs to be honest with one another and truly speak with one voice to the rest of the players in the sourcing engagement.

Steering Committee

The steering committee is composed of mid-level and senior-level associates from both the service provider and the customer. Although senior in stature, this group gets involved in delivery from a strategy-setting, escalation-resolving, and partner-supporting perspective. Some people should represent multiple groups. For example, we think it is critical for the customer-side CIO to be part of this group. The other customer-side people in this group should be the CFO, the BU head, and maybe the COO for a mid-sized company. On the service provider side, the client partner or the relationship manager, the practice heads, and the BU heads must be included in this group. Steering committees play a big role in managing the service provider's image within the customer community.

Program Management Office (PMO)

This is the most significant office within an outsourcing engagement. The PMO is responsible for owning the plan of record, coordinating multiple teams, managing program scope, communicating program status to multiple stakeholders, implementing training, and maintaining program schedules. We are convinced that, for large deals, the PMO role should be split between two individuals, the program managers from the customer and from the service provider. The delivery managers from the service provider should also be an integral part of this community.

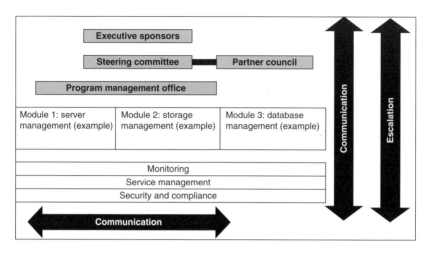

Figure 12.1 An Overview of the Big Deal Governance Model

Partner Council

Although viewed as an optional group by many service providers, we think that this group brings tremendous value to the table. Nine out of 10 times, most Big Deal deliveries include some component of dealing with outside vendors. This may mean software, hardware, and application vendors. When disputes arise because of the problems created by a vendor product, the triangulation of blame starts among the three parties: service provider, vendor (third party), and customer. This group is designed to help remove vendor-related roadblocks and facilitate vendor-relationship management with both the service provider and the customer. We think this group should consist of the service provider's client partner or relationship manager, the customer's head of IT (perhaps not a CIO in this case; someone at the vice president level will do), and senior representatives from all vendors. Vendors often put sales reps in this group, which is fine so long as they can resolve delivery-related disputes by mobilizing their organization. This group should meet at least once a month, via phone, to discuss aspects of partnership elements.

Figures 12.1 and 12.2 summarize our recommendations regarding large deal governance.

For large deal delivery, the service provider and the customer have to communicate with one another at every level. The communication should move sideways as well as up and down. The escalation

Responsibilities: What Does It Mean?	Roles: Who Are They?
Executive sponsors • Help champion the partnership • Strategic communication • Approve customization	Customer's chief information officer Customer's business sponsor Provider's executive sponsor
Steering committee • Represent strategy • Resolve escalations • Provide partnership support	Customer's chief information officer Customer's chief financial officer Customer's head of IT for different lines of businesses Provider's account management Provider's practice leaders Provider's principal relationship manager Provider's vertical leaders
Program management office • Own plan of record • Cross-team coordination • Manage scope • Drive training • Report program status • Own program schedule • Improve continuously	Customer's program manager Provider's onsite program manager Provider's offshore program manager
Partner council • Attend scheduled meetings with program management office • Resolve vendor-related issues	Third-party vendors Customer's head of IT Provider's principal relationship manager
Continuous improvement • Manage operational objectives • Ensure process synergies • Engage project champions	Provider's head of modules Provider's offshore program manager Provider's onsite program manager

Figure 12.2 Roles and Responsibilities in Big Deal Governance

mechanism should also be transparent and visible in order to resolve disputes.

We asked delivery leaders from six non-Indian global sourcing service providers and three service providers from India Inc. whether they feel their organization's governance structure incorporates an understanding of what the customer stakeholders want. We also asked if they feel their governance is based on partnering the customer at every level.

Not surprisingly, several of those interviewed told us that their organization takes appropriate measures to define the governance structure. A couple of the service providers were even proud that their governance programs have been created with the help of some top-notch strategy consulting companies; they were sure that all the customer agendas (CFO, CIO, and COO) had been taken into consideration in defining the governance structure. Supposing many large organizations do the right thing in setting up the structure, why do so many organizations fail to deliver large deals if all the processes and metrics are in place? We think it is because they have the wrong people managing the program and delivery. We believe every organization that is serious about running large deals successfully needs to invest heavily in one major role: a good onsite program manager.

What Makes a Good Program Manager?

Service-delivery organizations often do not really find appropriate people for these roles but promote people into them. Raj's story in Box 12.2 shows how service providers sometimes select program managers.

Box 12.2: The Not-So-Best Practice of Selecting a Program Manager

Raj is the program manager for a large Indian service-delivery provider. He started off as a software engineer in Chennai, India, and was quite good at it. As a reward, he was shipped to the U.S. for an on-site role. After a few years with the customer, working as a programmer and team lead, he was moved to a higher billing role as a project manager in the same account. He knew the customer well and had a good grasp of the work, so he had no problem in managing the work. He knew most of the code anyway, because he had written a lot of it.

After a few years at the customer site, he was thinking of leaving the job. This was partly because he had recently received his green card (permanent resident status in the U.S.) and was

(continued)

---

free to change employers as he deemed fit. It's sometimes difficult for employees using a work visa in the U.S. to switch employers. The service provider did not want to lose Raj. They offered him a better-paying job as a program manager with a manufacturing customer. Although he was not thrilled to relocate to Detroit from the Bay Area, Raj was excited that this job would help him get exposure in the car manufacturing industry. After all, he had been a high-tech lifer.

Four months into the job, Raj quit. His customer constantly complained about his inability to work with his team and get the job done. Also, he could not manage the office of the CFO, who ceaselessly grilled him about cutting costs, even after the contract was in place. The service provider was shocked by this outcome; Raj was treated as an employee in the previous account, where they loved him. Raj left the job and went back to the former account as an employee. His new role: technology architect.

Program management is the process of managing multiple ongoing projects in an organization. Program managers are like the army captains who mobilize the ground-level warfare operations in the field. Program managers have to continuously shepherd many project managers as well as the onsite and offshore delivery teams who are doing the work.

This explanation of the role of program manager accurately describes the role, but it fails to highlight the realities. Good program managers, managing large deals, bring a value to the table that is hard to teach. These leaders are exceptional politicians who know how to avoid the landmines in a customer organization. When they land a new gig, they are often handed an unpleasant surprise (see Box 12.3).

Box 12.3: When Chaos Awaits

John Decosta is a senior program manager with a major global sourcing provider. He has recently landed a major assignment as the program manager for a multibillion-dollar global customer in Silicon Valley. His company has worked long and hard to win this large deal, worth more than US$25 million. There is true potential

(continued)

to grow this account to more than US$50 million in the span of a few years. This is a strategic customer and all eyes from the VBU are on this account. The deal was sold on the guaranteed availability of John as program manager, a seasoned SAP functional consultant, and two solution architects. Everybody was expecting John to deliver results in exceptional fashion.

When the work started, reality hit. John was told that the SAP functional expert was not coming to the U.S., for personal reasons. The two solution architects did not get their H1-B visas (the non-immigrant visa to work in the U.S.) on time, so they could not be deployed on-site for a long period. John's first assignment was to smooth-talk the customer executives and explain to them how everything would be brought under control.

Although a smooth talker, John faced an uphill battle this time. The customer had been burned before by a major global player who over-charged and under-performed, sucking time and money from the customer. This time around, the customer planned to enforce the "no-nonsense" clause (camouflaged under legalese but basically giving the customer the right to easily kick the vendor off the project for non-performance) written into the SLA.

While John was letting this news about the unavailability of resources sink in before breaking it to the customers, he was greeted with more, equally shocking, news. He would also be responsible for managing several project managers who had never managed any projects before. His job would be to bring in business integration efficiencies by mobilizing these rookie leaders.

John's situation is not so unique. In today's world of fast-moving, highly competitive deliveries, service providers are forced to push the program managers to use every bit of efficiency in their operation. This is just a fancy way of saying "do more with less."

There are many good books about program management on the market. They teach high-quality best practices with operational models, but we have realized that once program managers actually hit the floor many of these best practices go straight out the window. Our experiences in this section are based on what actually works on the shop floor. We believe that good program managers need three basic skills to manage large deals successfully: collaborating, relaying expertise, and exuding authority.

Collaboration

We would say that 80 percent of the top program managers bring this first skill to the table. These leaders sometimes do not have technical or functional know-how about the projects. However, they can seamlessly work across the customer organization, the service-delivery units within the service provider organization, and the alliance organizations to drive results. Those program managers who are believers in the collaboration strategy are excellent at building consensus and kicking ass when needed, to get the work done. We recommend this type of leadership if you are interested in driving large programs where you may not have the required functional or technical skills.

Expertise

We would say that only a small percentage of program managers rely on this skill set. They may have been superior in a functional area or a technology area and later graduated into managing projects and programs in those areas. They act as *de facto* SMEs and are able to influence teams because of their accepted credibility. It is hard to be an expert in many things, and program managers relying on this skill may be of limited use for the service provider.

Authority

Have you ever run into leaders who can get things done just by using their charm? Or how about those top bosses whose emails simply get the work done? There is a small community of program managers who are able to influence teams because of their perceived or real authority.

But simply having these traits is not enough. Program managers are often faced with the difficult challenge of getting work done by way of the customer's resources. Many of these people are executives who are on a much higher level of pay than the program manager's pay grade. We have seen many program managers fail because they simply cannot influence the customer's people to do their part. This challenge also exists in mobilizing the service provider's employees as well. In today's vertical (BU) and horizontal (competency) business models, nothing is really stopping an architect reporting to a horizontal and thereby flipping the finger to the program manager.

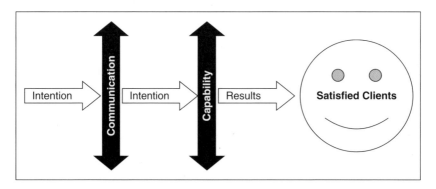

Figure 12.3 Person Commitment and Capability model

Sandip Bhattacharya is a senior program manager at a major IT service provider. For sixteen years, he has managed large enterprise SAP projects in the U.S., Europe, and India. Sandip has a unique take on how to manage the situation when customer or service provider employees are not doing the work. He basically judges the actions of all his stakeholders through the lens of the model seen in Figure 12.3. This is a model he created, based on his experience of working with numerous personality profiles. This model can be used for any management situation, but program managers will often have an opportunity to use it. The next section of the chapter embodies Sandip's unique take on program management, which we found to be spot-on.

Prior to work being given to a team member (who could be from the customer or the service provider), a good program manager should judge whether this person has the intention, and the desire, to do the work. Program managers need to play pop psychologist in assessing intention, throughout the duration of the engagement. During the engagement, intention should be demonstrated via action. Simple intention without action is just as bad as having no intention. We have all seen situations where good people suddenly slack off. Instead of taking a drop in performance at face value, good program managers need to take a deeper look to understand the cause of the drop. Did he or she lose interest in the work? Or is the person just not capable of handling what is being done? Is the person trying hard but failing? Basically, the goal is to find out the level of commitment and the resulting action, or lack thereof. If people are bored out of their minds and don't want to do the work, they need to be handled differently from a person who simply cannot code Java to save his or her life. If the person who is slacking off because of boredom is losing commitment, maybe a promise to move him to another project in the near future will restore his commitment. But if you, as a program manager, cannot get a person to be committed and action-driven for the mission, regardless of the cause, you need to get this person off the team as soon as possible. This remains true regardless of who you are dealing with, whether it's a customer or a team member from your own company. Obviously, in the real world, we all get stuck with team members who may pull us down. But at the very least, you should notify your client partner or relationship manager about it.

Actions need to end in positive results. If you have a person who tries hard, staying late at night to do work but not able to complete coding, then that person is not producing results. If it is because of some technical or functional incapability, then give the person some time to improve. An effective program manager has to learn the balance between being a drill sergeant and a compassionate monk, at the drop of a dime.

Figure 12.3 shows the model pictorially.

Conclusion

Managing large programs requires a thorough understanding of the customers' needs. This includes understanding the needs of the multiple BU leaders (COO needs), the bean counters (CFO needs), and the IT leaders (CIO needs). If you are proposing a governance model that does not yield results satisfying the needs of all these stakeholders, then you are in trouble. The governance model also has to be modular because this helps break work into functional chunks. The model must have a way to foster communication across the whole program. For every major grouping within the governance model, there should be participation from both the customer and the service provider. The *mantra* of shared responsibility and outcome should be ingrained among all team members, both customer and service provider employees alike.

Program managers need to be true leaders, using a collaborative attitude to get things done. As a leader, if you have to deal with a person who has low commitment but high capability yet refuses to change course and be committed, kick him or her out of the engagement. Conversely, if you have a person on the team with high commitment but little capability, then be patient. Give the person some training.

Finally, most of the people you will lead as a program manager will have mid-level commitment and capability. Our suggestion is to keep them in the engagement but watch and guide them carefully to ensure progress.

A simple market has a few goods and services that allow merchants to barter like-for-like without fanfare or obstacles. In a more complex market where *specialty* products and services are offered by multiple competitors, each seeking to capture the buyer's spendable currency or other assets in trade, the relationships and wealth move around dynamically and end up in the hands of those who have managed to give the *best value, lowest total cost, highest quality, and highest return on net assets.*

We want thank you for reading this book. We have tried to capture our thoughts, which are based on our practical experience on the sell side of doing big global sourcing deals. We hope that you have learned about the entire pursuit cycle and are better prepared to go and bid for your next Big Deal.

Some Parting Thoughts

This book would not be complete if we did not present some views on the deal-making profession itself. As we journeyed through the book, we covered the entire global sourcing Big Deals spectrum. Big Deals are won with the help of many people representing multiple groups. We have specifically addressed certain sales-related job roles: relationship manager, account manager, client executive, and business development executive (in Chapter Three) and semi-sales roles such as TPA relationship manager (in Chapter Four). We have also discussed technology service delivery responsibilities such as transition management, program management, and service delivery management (in Chapters Eleven and Twelve). But when one thinks about the deal-making team in the context of global sourcing, one typically refers to the specific individuals who are part of the core commercial negotiation team. Read the section "Assembling the 'Dream Team' of Large Deal Negotiators" in Chapter Nine for details about the core negotiation team.

The core strength of global sourcing Big Deals team members lies in putting the entire scope of the deal in the context of legal, commercial (finance and pricing), and what we like to call "business terms." This last phrase is a broad paint brush that covers understanding business domain competency, technology competency, sales evangelism, transition, and governance for the entire deal. Here is a quick career guide for your reference.

- *Deal director* If you want to be a deal director, you need to have an overall deep (not necessarily specialized) understanding of the entire Big Deals pursuit process. As a generalist, you also have to possess a fairly deep level of knowledge in legal, pricing, and business terms. People with a sales management, project management, or process-oriented background tend to become good deal directors. Because this role requires a lot of leading from the rear, many frontline sales people transitioning into this role find it difficult to adjust; they may believe that they are not getting due credit for their achievements. We have dedicated an entire chapter (Five) to leading from the rear.

- *Pricing (financial) strategist* This is a pure finance MBA type of job. You need very good knowledge of finance. You should be able to create different cost and pricing models, supported by a business case. It's always a plus to have some knowledge about corporate tax and law to be good at this role. This role is not simply a back-end analytical role. You must also have the conversation skills to persuade both internal and external stakeholders about your financial prescriptions.

- *Commercial (legal) strategist* Generally, lawyers with outsourcing law experience or professionals with contract management background are ideal candidates for this role. This role requires thorough understanding of country-specific laws regarding labor and business. Commercial strategists are also well versed in understanding how a contract may change because of changes in financial structuring. Some commercial strategists also know tax law well.

- *Solution architect* We are talking about high-level technology gurus here. Solution architects have a good technology architecture background across multiple technologies. They should also have good understanding of domain-centric solutions that are prevalent in a number of industries. Solution architects are extremely well versed in analyzing the real scope of work and prescribing a solution by looking at the RFP. Former technology consultants, class architects, and software engineers with knowledge across multiple technologies and businesses are good candidates for graduating into this role. Sometimes, solution architects are not directly part of the deals team but represent the VBUs or are part of the corporate solutions group.

Besides the specific skills mentioned here, all these roles require good traditional negotiation skills; the soft skill of calmly and rationally working point by point through the contract and moving the deal toward closure. The good thing about Big Deal negotiation is that it is a learned skill. One can always take some negotiation classes at a company, private institute, or university to learn the basic skills. The best way to learn negotiation, however, is to follow the *mantra* of time-tested medical surgeons: "See one, do one, teach one." If you are an observer in a live Big Deal negotiation, you will learn more about negotiation than any formal class can offer. Unfortunately, we have not come across a lot of negotiating experts extending this opportunity to freshmen negotiators. A few instances of being an observer will give you the confidence to be a negotiator yourself in a Big Deal, and as you graduate into doing negotiations your skills and confidence will just get better. Veteran negotiators can also sharpen their saws by conducting debriefing sessions with the rookie observers and going over in detail the just-concluded negotiation. This see one, do one, teach one approach to grooming negotiators may help your organization in winning future Big Deals.

There is no hard-and-fast requirement or rule on exactly how to get into the deal team roles mentioned here. If you feel that you possess the required attributes and experience to be successful, then you should pursue these roles within a number of service providers. Most large global service providers have deal-making roles even if they do not have a dedicated group doing Big Deals.

Deal team members earn a handsome living. They travel all over the world, live in elite hotels, and are on the frequent flier list of many of the world's top airlines. But here comes the caveat. Is this profession right for you? Deal makers are on the road a lot, sometimes close to 100 percent of the time. Long work hours are common. It is not unheard of for us in this profession to work on a proposal throughout a flight from Chicago to New Delhi (yes, in today's business climate it's in Economy class) and walk straight into a late-night team meeting in the Indian capital preparing for the next day's face-to-face commercial negotiation with the customer. Before you embark on this profession, you should ask yourself, "Am I ready to miss my child's birthday and not be able to ever take her to soccer practice? Is my spouse or significant other OK with the fact that I may have to cancel our long-planned family vacation because a Big Deal has just surfaced? Am I also willing to carry an enormous sales target every year knowing very well that I am dependent on the sales teams to uncover the deals for me? And most of the time, am I the one who is walking the tightrope of making the business units and corporate happy in a deal when everybody has differing agendas?" But if you decide to pursue this challenging career as a Big Deal maker, we believe that you will become part of a small fraternity of people who enjoy the ultimate job satisfaction: euphoria coupled with the pride that comes from securing a massive win.

INDEX

A

ABN AMRO 7
Accenture 9, 11, 18, 44, 189
account development 38–41, 49
account manager 33, 38, 39, 40, 41, 42, 55
ACE 71
advanced deal structuring 105, 118, 154
alliance 17, 65, 99, 111, 113–116, 210
Alsbridge 58
alternative dispute resolution (ADR)
    145–147
AMEX 103
analyzing deal wish list 91
Anti-celebrity 76
application 4, 19, 44, 73, 93, 112, 113, 117,
    132, 134, 154, 169, 185, 186, 196, 205
arbitration 145, 147
Arthur Andersen 9
Ascension Health 4
Asia 24, 52, 73, 169
asset 11, 44, 59, 69, 89, 94, 95, 97, 102, 120,
    123, 143, 150, 153, 157, 158, 159, 183,
    185, 213
asset valuation 150
Atos Origin 11
ATT 4
attitude 9, 13, 20, 21, 22, 52, 71, 84, 118,
    200
authority 19, 40, 42, 61, 69, 74, 209–212
Aviva Global Services 115

B

Bakshi Nirmal (Nimma) 111
Balanced Performance 38
Balu T. 25, 27
benchmark 56, 61, 89, 93, 96, 97, 105, 106,
    135–137, 174, 189, 201
best practices 12, 14, 36, 38, 42, 49, 98,
    100, 101, 108, 138–144, 157–162, 182,
    187, 209
Bhattacharya Sandip 211

Bhupathi, Mahesh 14, 195
bid 12, 13, 19, 20, 21, 23–25, 28, 60, 62, 64,
    71, 80, 84, 88–91, 98–100, 102, 104, 105,
    107, 161, 170, 171, 172, 182, 198, 213
Big Deal engagement model 93–96
Big Deal lifecycle 11
Big Deals 4–9, 11–13, 33–41, 61, 62, 87, 91,
    94, 96, 99, 105, 106, 115, 127, 129, 132,
    133, 144–147, 149, 150, 151, 152, 154,
    161, 162, 167, 171, 173, 181, 195, 198
billing rate 97, 150
binding agent 75, 76
Bird and Bird 58
Blackman, Lori 28, 29
body shopping 94
Bose, Subhas Chandra 26
BPO 88, 100, 115, 143
Brazil 10, 61, 116, 197
British Telecom 4, 105
broad-based networks 37–41
Brown, Doug xvi
BT Concert 4
bundled and mixed pricing 99, 101
build-operate-own-transfer (BOOT) 115
build-operate-transfer (BOT) 115, 116,
    117
business development 34, 49, 51
business development executive 33, 34,
    42
business-process modeling 58
business transformation 4, 186
business unit (BU) 5, 6, 9, 12, 17, 19, 23,
    24, 49, 53, 56, 62–64, 69, 74, 77–80, 89,
    92, 98, 99, 106, 112, 123, 130, 141, 152,
    153, 154, 167, 168, 169, 175, 176, 199,
    204, 210, 212

C

Capgemini 11, 18
capture executive 151, 152
case study 116, 117, 167–177